Passionate Leadership in Education

Passionate Leadership in Education

Edited by
Brent Davies and Tim Brighouse

Los Angeles • London • New Delhi • Singapore

SAGE Publications Ltd
1 Oliver's Yard
55 City Road
London EC1Y 1SP

SAGE Publications Inc.
2455 Teller Road
Thousand Oaks, California 91320

SAGE Publications India Pvt Ltd
B 1/I 1 Mohan Cooperative Industrial Area
Mathura Road, Post Bag 7
New Delhi 110 044

SAGE Publications Asia-Pacific Pte Ltd
33 Pekin Street #02-01
Far East Square
Singapore 048763

Library of Congress Control Number: 2008921690
British Library Cataloguing in Publication data

A catalogue record for this book is available from the British Library

ISBN 978-1-4129-4861-6
ISBN 978-1-4129-4862-3 (pbk)

Typeset by Dorwyn, Wells, Somerset
Printed in Great Britain by TJ International Ltd, Padstow, Cornwall
Printed on paper from sustainable resources

Mixed Sources
Product group from well-managed
forests and other controlled sources
www.fsc.org Cert no. SGS-COC-2482
© 1996 Forest Stewardship Council
FSC

Dedication

To: Tim Bristow, Berta Bustorff, David Gifford, David Lamper, Gill Metcalfe, Seamus O'Donovan, Julie Roberts, Barbara Stern, Alan Thomas and Graham Wright in recognition in of their passion for success

Contents

Editors and contributors

Editors

Dr Brent Davies is Professor of Leadership Development at the University of Hull. He is also a Professorial Fellow at the University of Melbourne, a Special Professor at the University of Nottingham, a Visiting Professor at the Institute of Education (University of London) and a Faculty Member of the Centre on Educational Governance at the University of Southern California. He is an associate director of the Specialist Schools and Academies Trust. Brent spent the first ten years of his career working as a teacher in South London. He then moved into higher education and now works exclusively on leadership and management development programmes for senior and middle managers in schools. Brent was Head of Education Leadership at Crewe+Alsager College of Higher Education and then moved to be the Director of the International MBA in School Leadership at Leeds Metropolitan University. He then moved to the University of Lincolnshire and Humberside to establish the first Chair in Educational Leadership and create the International Educational Leadership Centre in Lincoln. He moved to the University of Hull in 2000 to establish the International Leadership Centre. In 2004 he moved within the University to become a Research Professor in Leadership Development at the Hull University Business School.

He has published extensively, with 21 books and 80 articles on leadership and management. His recent books include: *Developing Sustainable Leadership* (Sage, 2007); *Strategic Marketing for Schools*

(Beijing Normal University Press, 2007); *Leading the Strategically Focused School* (Sage, 2006); *Naujoji Strategine Kryptis Ir Mokyklos Pletre* (Vilnus: Homo libre, 2006); *The Essentials of School Leadership* (Sage, 2005); *School Leadership in the 21st Century* (Routledge, 2005), *The New Strategic Direction and Development of the School* (Routledge-Falmer, 2003), *The Handbook of Educational Leadership and Management* (Pearson, 2003).

Tim Brighouse is Visiting Professor at the Institute of Education in London having recently retired from being first Commissioner and then Chief Adviser for London Schools. Before that he was for ten years Chief Education Officer for Birmingham and spent another decade as Chief Education Officer for Oxfordshire. In between he was Professor of Education at Keele University for four years and earlier taught in Derbyshire and South Wales before entering educational administration and working in Monmouthshire, Buckinghamshire and the Inner London Education Authority. Tim has written several books including *What makes a good school?*, *How to improve your school*, *The essential pieces in the jigsaw of the successful school* and *How successful headteachers survive and thrive,* as well as articles for newspapers and magazines, including the *Political Quarterly*, the *Oxford Review of Education* as well as the broadsheets and educational press.

Contributors

Dr Brian J. Caldwell is Managing Director of Educational Transformations Pty Ltd in Melbourne and Associate Director of International Networking for Educational Transformation (iNet) (Global) of the Specialist Schools and Academies Trust in England. From 1998 to 2004 he served as Dean of Education at the University of Melbourne where he is currently Professorial Fellow. His previous appointments include Head of Education Policy and Management (1995–1998) at the University of Melbourne where he took up an appointment in 1990; and Head of Teacher Education (1988–1999) and Dean of Education (1989–1990) at the University of Tasmania. His international work over the last 25 years includes more than 450 presentations, projects and other professional assignments in or for

38 countries or jurisdictions on six continents. In addition to more than 100 published papers, chapters and monographs, Brian Caldwell is author or co-author of books that helped guide educational reform in several countries, most notably the trilogy on self-managing schools: *The Self-Managing School* (1988), *Leading the Self-Managing School* (1992) and *Beyond the Self-Managing School* (1998), each with Jim Spinks. *Re-imagining Educational Leadership* was published in 2006. *Raising the Stakes: From Improvement to Transformation in the Reform of Schools* (2008) is his fourth collaboration with Jim Spinks.

Christopher Day is Professor of Education and Director of the Teacher and Leadership Research Centre (TLRC). Prior to this he worked as a teacher, lecturer and local education authority adviser. He is editor of *Teachers and Teaching: Theory and Practice*. He is currently directing a twelve-country project on successful school principalship; a nine-country European project on successful principalship in schools in challenging urban contexts; and national projects on school leadership and pupil outcomes; and effective classroom teaching. His books have been published in several languages and include *Teachers Matter* (Open University Press, 2007); *Successful Principal Leadership in Times of Change: An International Perspective* (Springer, 2007); *A Passion for Teaching* (Falmer, 2004); *International Handbook on the Continuing Professional Development of Teachers* (Open University Press, 2004); and *Developing Teachers: The Challenges of Lifelong Learning* (Falmer Press, 1999).

Alan Flintham was for 15 years a secondary school headteacher in Nottinghamshire, until retiring on age-related grounds in 2005. He is now an Education Consultant and a Research Associate of the National College for School Leadership, having published reports on 'Reservoirs of Hope: spiritual and moral leadership in head-teachers' (2003), 'When Reservoirs Run Dry: Why Some Headteachers Leave Headship Early' (2003), and 'What's Good About Leading Schools in Challenging Circumstances' (2006). He was awarded a Churchill Fellowship to visit Australia in 2005 to study how school principals are formed and developed in that country. He has been involved in the setting up and evaluation of a recently developed peer support scheme for Nottinghamshire head-

teachers, and has significant experience of mentoring and supporting both newly qualified and experienced colleagues from all phases
and social contexts of schools. He is a Research Fellow of Liverpool
Hope University where he is continuing his research into school
leadership and what supports and sustains it.

Dr Andy Hargreaves is the Thomas More Brennan Chair in Education
at the Lynch School of Education, Boston College. Prior to that, he
was Professor of Educational Leadership and Change at the University of Nottingham, England and Co-Director of and Professor in
the International Centre for Educational Change at the Ontario
Institute for Studies in Education, University of Toronto. His most
recent book, co-authored with Dean Fink, is *Sustainable Leadership*,
(Jossey Bass, 2006).

John MacBeath is the Professor Emeritus at the University of
Cambridge and until 2000 was Director of the Quality in Education
Centre at the University of Strathclyde in Glasgow. From 1997 to
2001 he was a member of the Government's Task Force on
Standards, and from 1997 to 1999 of Scotland's Action Group
Standards. Other consultancies have included OECD, UNESCO and
International Labour Organisation (ILO), the Bertelsmann Founda-
tion and the European Commission. He is currently a consultant on
self-evaluation and inspection in Hong Kong and is Chair of the
Hong Kong based International Network for Educational Improve-
ment. He is President of the International Congress on School
Effectiveness and Improvement and is Director of Leadership for
Learning at the Cambridge Network. He has written widely on
school self-evaluation, school improvement and school leadership.
In 1997 he received the OBE for services to education.

Dr John M. Novak is a Professor of Education at Brock University,
Canada, where he has been Chair of Graduate Studies in Education,
Chair of the University Faculty Board, and a member of the Board
of Trustees. He is the Past-President of the Society of Professors of
Education and is on the Board of Trustees of the International
Alliance for Invitational Education. As co-founder of Invitational
Education (with William Purkey), he has been an active writer and
speaker on the inviting school movement. His books authored,

co-authored, and edited include *Fundamentals of Invitational Education* (2008), *Creating Inviting Schools* (2006), *Inviting Educational Leadership* (2002), *Inviting School Success,*(1996) *Democratic Teacher Education* (1994), and *Advancing Invitational Thinking* (1992). As an invited keynote speaker, he has addressed groups on six continents, from Honduras to Hong Kong, and from north of the Arctic Circle to the bottom of New Zealand. He is currently working on the 4th edition of *Inviting School Success*, a follow-up to *Inviting Educational Leadership*, a book, *From Conflict to Conciliation*, and a publication, with his daughter, Natalie, *Appreciating the Human Perspective*. In addition, after 36 years of thrashing around in the water as a certified basic SCUBA diver, he finally earned his Advanced Underwater Diving Certification.

Dr Geoff Southworth is Deputy Chief Executive and Strategic Director of Research and Policy at the National College for School Leadership (NCSL). He began his career as a teacher in Lancashire, where he taught in three schools before becoming headteacher of a school in Leyland. During his headship he became involved in school management training programmes which prompted him to move into higher education in Cambridge. At the Cambridge Institute (later School of Education) he directed management courses for headteachers, deputies and middle leaders. In 1997 he was appointed Professor of Education at the University of Reading. He has written many articles and chapters in books, as well as authoring, co-authoring or editing 14 books. He has also conducted a number of school-based research projects investigating school leadership and school improvement. In 2002 he moved to the NCSL to become the Director for Research. He was and continues to be responsible for the strategic direction of the College's research and evaluation activities. In 2005 he was promoted to Deputy CEO, working closely with the CEO and the strategic and operational directors. He was awarded an OBE for services to education in the 2008 New Years Honours.

Passionate leadership

Brent Davies

Passionate leadership is about energy, commitment, a belief that every child can learn and will learn, a concern with social justice and the optimism that we can make a difference. It takes leadership from the realm of a role or job to one of an abiding drive to enhance children's learning and children's lives. What is it that makes some leaders so passionate about their leadership role that they inspire their staff and transform children's lives?

Passion is often seen in terms of a passion for social justice, passion for learning, passion to make a difference. It is the passion to make a difference that turns beliefs into reality and is the mark of deep leadership. Beliefs are statements or views that help us set our personal views and experiences into context. Passion works on the emotional side of leadership. Bolman and Deal (1995: 12) in their inspirational book *Leading with Soul* emphasize the emotional side of leadership:

> *Heart, hope and faith, rooted in soul and spirit, are necessary for today's managers to become tomorrows' leaders, for today's sterile bureaucracies to become tomorrow's communities of meaning ...*

Passion must be the driving force that moves vision into action. Bennis and Nanus (1985: 92–93) use a now classic definition to argue that the creation of a sense of meaning is one of the distinguishing features of leadership:

1

> *The leader operates on the emotional and spiritual resources of the organisation, on its values, commitment, and aspirations ... leaders often inspire their followers to high levels of achievement by showing them how their work contributes to worthwhile ends. It is an emotional appeal to some of the most fundamental of human needs – the need to be important, to make a difference, to feel useful, to be part of a successful and worthwhile enterprise.*

Passionate leadership establishes a set of values and purposes that underpin the educational process in the school. Most significantly it is the individual passion and commitment of the leader that drives the values and purposes into reality. Values without implementation do little for the school. It is in the tackling of difficult challenges to change and improve, often by confronting unacceptable practices, that passionate leaders show their educational values.

What skill does deep leadership require to translate passion into reality? This book brings together a number of outstanding leadership writers to voice key ideas and concepts about what makes leaders passionate in their role and their schools. How can we capture that unique leadership ability to change all those around them by their undimmable optimism and deep value system to meet the challenges of day-to-day management and rise above it with passionate leadership?

After 1988 which ushered in a market forces in education, headteachers, were for a few years, encouraged to be managers or chief executives. It was their job, so they were told, to manage the introduction of the national curriculum and demonstrate they could manage functions formerly carried out on their behalf by the Local Education Authority (LEA). They were suddenly, if indirectly, exposed to the prevailing management wisdoms of the business world.

By the mid 1990s, however, a few LEAs were encouraging headteachers to 'lead' their schools on a journey of improvement. To do that successfully would require a focus on what went on in the classroom. The incoming Labour government of 1997 seized on and encouraged this focus even though they mandated on schools a plethora of change, which required considerable management as well as leadership skills.

By 2008, the accountability culture has become oppressive with targets and delivery of 'shallow learning' as demonstrated by the testing culture seriously damaging 'deep' educational purpose and understanding. How do headteachers in this culture manage one side of the coin, which is deliver targets and the other, be passionate about education and the enhancement of human potential?

To meet this challenge we have drawn on outstanding writers and researchers in the leadership field to show how this passion survives and prospers, and is a moral driving force in ensuring children becoming all they can become. That brings me to the other thing about our definition of passionate school leadership: for us it's a passion to change things for the better, a passion with a moral foundation. In reading the following chapters we hope that leaders in education will use it to reframe and reignite their own passion for learning and education, which is at the cornerstone of all they do.

Editing a book with Tim Brighouse has provided me with a unique opportunity to work with one of my educational heroes. Indeed when I suggested we develop some ideas on passionate leadership it became clear that Tim was 'passionate leadership' personified! His leadership, which has spanned several decades, has been unique in preserving and articulating educational values and educational purpose in an era of managerialism and accountability where many educational officers were being replaced by accountability bureaucrats. Tim has been the role model for educational values; it has been a privilege working with him.

This book has been structured in five major sections.

- The first section is concerned with defining the passionate teacher, the passionate leader and the passionate school, with the core chapter by Tim Brighouse.
- The second section centres on passion and educational leadership, with chapters from John Novak and Alan Flintham.
- The third section looks at research on passionate leadership, with chapters from Chris Day and Brent Davies.
- The fourth section considers passionate leadership for schools and teachers, with chapters from John MacBeath and Andy Hargreaves.
- The fifth section centres on defining the work of passionate leaders and building a model for passionate leadership, with chapters from Geoff Southworth and Brian Caldwell.

I will briefly outline each chapter.

In Chapter 1, Tim Brighouse writes persuasively on three themes: passionate teachers; passionate leaders and passionate schools. Using leadership stories and case examples he provides a rich picture of what passionate and outstanding leaders, and schools are like. In looking at the beliefs of passionate and outstanding teachers he provides values to which we all would aspire for teachers. He lists these five values as (i) the transformability rather than the fixed or predictable ability of those they teach; (ii) success is possible and expected for all pupils and a failure to learn immediately is a challenge to their own teaching, not a sign of the pupil's inability to learn; (iii) intelligence/talent is multifaceted rather than general and indicated by speed in problem-solving, literacy and numeracy; (iv) a child showing great effort to learn is a sign of strong character not of limited ability to learn; (v) all the children they teach need a worthwhile relationship with at least one adult, who may not be them.

He moves on to passionate leaders and what they do, using powerful leadership role modelling of headteachers who are credible examples of learners and teachers as well as being effective and inspiring storytellers of the events and values of the school. He goes on to consider that passionate leaders are good delegators and risk takers. They also have the ability to create capacity and energy among staff. He also sees passionate leaders as seeking and charting improvement while meeting and minimizing crisis. In the final part of his chapter, Tim looks at the characteristics of passionate schools, the heart of which he sees as 'values'. It is clear that Tim's values and passions run throughout the chapter.

In Chapter 2, John Novak develops his ideas on passionate leadership by taking the conceptual frame of 'inviting' by setting his ideas in the title of inviting passionate leadership. To quote John, 'this chapter will present an inviting approach to educational leadership that seeks to call forth passion and discernment. Based on the idea that it is essential for educational leaders to care about passion and be passionate about caring'. In answering the question 'passionate about what?' John takes the perspective that in an inviting approach leaders are passionate about five concepts: (i) people are valuable, able and responsible and should be treated accordingly; (ii) the process of educating should be a collaborative, cooperative activity; (iii) the process, the way we go about doing something, is the product in the making; (iv) all people possess untapped potential in all areas of worthwhile human endeavour; (v) this potential can be realized by places, policies, programmes, and processes designed to invite development and by people who are intentionally inviting with themselves and others personally and professionally.

The articulation by John of these keys ideas clearly recognizes it is desirable to subscribe to these ideas but how do we witness this passion acting out in practice? He puts forward that this passion for education needs to be seen in the way that leaders interact with people, places, policies, programmes and processes. Finally John argues that we need to sustain passionate leadership and leaders.

In Chapter 3, Alan Flintham argues that successful leaders often act as 'external reservoirs of hope' for the school and its staff as it strives to deliver its vision while facing many external pressures. The school community looks to the headteacher to provide the hope that will sustain it to translate that vision with passion and drive it into reality. Alan questions that while the headteacher provides that external reservoir of hope in keeping true to the ideal that the school will be successful, who provides the support to the headteacher? For headteachers to maintain their passion and drive for the school's success they need to draw on an internal reservoir of hope. What sustains that internal reservoir so that the internal passion does not die?

Alan argues that there are two imperatives: one a generational imperative based on the individual leaders' values that have been laid down through their life experience which gives them a 'passion to make a difference'. This is coupled with an egalitarian imperative which is the passion to see every child realize the potential they have and 'the school's job is to realize that potential'. In using the metaphor of the reservoirs, Alan discusses what drains the reservoir and what refills it and how headteachers can draw on support to rebuild drive and passion. Alan concludes with a discussion on the privilege and price of headship. This work is based on a unique research project for the National College for School Leadership and the leadership voices and experiences of the headteachers shine through the chapter.

In Chapter 4, Chris Day reports on research regarding the passion that drives headteachers to succeed in challenging circumstances.

His research reports that for the headteachers in his study, being passionate generates energy, determination, conviction, commitment and even obsession in people. He argues that passion is not a luxury, a frill, or a quality possessed by just a few headteachers, but it is essential to all successful leadership. The passion of the headteachers was expressed both through their enthusiasm, but also through principled, values-led leadership. Like effective teachers, these headteachers had a passion for their schools, a passion for their pupils and a passionate belief that who they were and how they led could make a difference in the lives of staff, pupils, parents and the community, both in the moments of leadership and in the days, weeks, months and even years afterwards.

Chris structures his chapter to consider how these headteachers had: a passion for achievement; a passion for care; a passion for collaboration; a passion for commitment; a passion for trust and a passion for inclusivity. Throughout the chapter the text is immensely enriched with the leadership voices of the headteachers in the research. This gives real and significant insights to what drives and motivates headteachers in challenging educational and social environments.

In Chapter 5, Brent Davies reports on passionate leadership in action drawing on research undertaken on leadership in the new Academies set up in recent years. By researching the leadership skills, characteristics and perspectives of Principals he reports on what drives these leaders to take on these challenging roles. Leading Academies in areas of social deprivation, school underperformance and often with local political hostility requires both passion for the challenge and the personal characteristics to stay the course!

Using the leadership voices of the Academy Principals the chapter outlines five key factors about their leadership in that they: (i) are passionate leaders – driven by the centrality of social justice and moral purpose; (ii) have an absolute passion for transformation of learning outcomes; (iii) a passion for sustainability by balancing the operational and strategic; (iv) are passionate about creating a 'sense of place' for learning; (v) passion is useless unless Principals have the personal characteristics to stay the course! The chapter seeks to isolate the leadership factors that can be used for the enhancement and development of senior leadership in new and challenging environments.

In Chapter 6, John MacBeath begins by noting that 'passionate leadership is not easy to pinpoint within the pressured environment of schools driven by targets and performance tables'. He moves on to argue that as well as a passion to oppose oppressive accountability environments, passion is manifested in leadership in a number of positive ways.

First among these is a passion for learning. John uses a powerful quotation from Jerry Starratt: 'the learning agenda of the school must connect to the moral agenda of the learners ... namely the agenda of finding and choosing and fashioning themselves as individuals and a human community.' (Starratt, 2005: 3). This passion is developed in a 'hidden passion' with teachers as leaders and learners. Their leadership is not just responding to external change but an internal change driven by the leaders' passion of 'being for' change that is a school directed to improve children's lives. The passion for student learning can be witnessed by the development of 'student voice' in the learning progress. John concludes his discussion by arguing that if we are passionate about education then developing the learning school would be a passionate outcome.

In Chapter 7, Andy Hargreaves, while not directly having researched the emotions of leaders, has done considerable work on the emotions of teaching. To consider the teacher perspective on passionate leadership Andy coins the phrase 'emotional geographies of educational leadership'. In setting out this conceptualization he uses five 'geographies': moral geographies, political geographies, cultural geographies, professional geographies and physical geographies. He argues that passionate leaders need to utilize emotional intelligence to understand the impact their leadership has on teachers.

In Chapter 8, Geoff Southworth undertakes a very significant review of what school leaders do and what makes them passionate about the job. Drawing on research from the National College for School Leadership (NCSL), he articulates that the major issues facing the profession are relentlessness, accountability and complexity of headship. In this chapter Geoff outlines what headship looks like today and links it to passionate leadership in terms of the leaders' energy, commitment and beliefs. Geoff draws on the work of Ken Leithwood (Leithwood et al., 2006; NCSL, 2007) to put forward the view that successful leaders are 'optimistic, have a vision for the school and a sense of mission in their work'.

In thinking about how headteachers can be enabled to be even more effective today and tomorrow, Geoff puts forward six ideas to: (i) improve leadership preparation and development; (ii) improve support for school leaders; (iii) accentuate the positive; (iv) move away from heroic headship; (v) examine values and visions; and (vi) encourage leaders to share their values. He goes on to suggest the personal characteristics which can be listed for effective leadership are, strength of character, humility, humour, optimism and passion.

In Chapter 9, Brian Caldwell both extends some of the analysis of what inspires headteachers used by Geoff Southworth in what he calls 'enchanting leadership', but then moves on to 'break new ground' to construct a unique and inspirational model of enchanted leadership. Brian makes an important distinction between 'enchanted leadership', the emotional response of the leader to the role, and 'enchanting leadership' which also includes the emotional responses of others to the leader. In modelling enchanting leadership Brian sets up two models to establish what makes enchanting leadership possible. The first is the 'internal relationships' of passion, trust and strategy that come together with a compelling vision driven by high moral purpose to achieve enchanting leadership. The second model is to enable the leader to see the 'bigger picture' beyond the immediate work setting to link education, the economy and society if leadership is to be enchanting.

Brian develops the ideas from this conceptualization by describing enchanting leadership in action, using political and educational leaders. Developing the theme that enchanting leadership must have a purpose, Brian considers how enchanting leadership contributes to the transformation of schools. For this he articulates a final model that links intellectual capital, social capital, financial capital and spiritual capital as means of improving student learning. He concludes with enchanting leadership as capital in the transformation of schools.

Conclusion

Leaders in schools today operate in challenging environments with results-driven accountability frameworks that can often conflict deeper educational values. How do they manage to balance these short-term demands with longer-term educational values and approaches? How do they sustain themselves and their staff in this environment and remain passionate about their education vision and mission? This book provides a set of fascinating insights into how leaders in our schools remain passionate and committed to the success of all our children.

References

Bennis, W. and Nanus, B. (1985) *Leaders*. New York: Harper Row.

Bolman, L. and Deal, T. E. (1995) *Leading with Soul*. San Francisco, CA: Jossey-Bass.

Leithwood, K., Day, C., Sammons, P., Harris, A. and Hopkins, D., (2006) *Seven Strong Claims About Successful School Leadership*. Nottingham: NCSL and DfES.

NCSL, (2007) *What we know about school leadership*. Nottingham: NCSL.

Starratt, R. J. (2005) 'The Ethics of Learning: An absent focus in the discourse on educational leadership'. Paper presented to the ILERN Group, Boston College, October.

Core ideas about passionate teachers, leaders and schools

Chapter 1

The passionate teacher and the passionate leader in the passionate school

Tim Brighouse

It is the thesis of this chapter that for a school to be outstandingly successful and to have that purposeful buzz about it that everyone recognizes and might qualify it to earn the sobriquet 'passionate', you need teachers who are themselves passionate and, for that to happen to a sufficient and lasting extent, they in turn will need passionate leadership. The evidence rests on stories from schools and recent conversations with ten headteachers all of whom recognized the issue of 'passion' in schooling as one worth discussing. As one of them remarked: 'The absence of it need not be disastrous – I have a perfectly efficient head of science who isn't passionate but gets results – but its presence provides a step-change in what's possible. Suddenly, things you always thought just out of reach are brought within your grasp.' But as this quote also identifies the crucial need for high competence allied to such passion: indeed if you are doomed to have the one without the other, competence is to be more highly prized.

A clue as to what one might mean is to be found in the following extract from Robert Fried's (2002) book *The Passionate Teacher*:

> *Of some of our teachers we remember their foibles, their mannerisms, of others their kindness and encouragement, or their fierce devotion to standards of work we probably didn't share at the time. But of those we remember most, we remember what they cared about and that they cared about us and the person we might become. It's this quality of caring about ideas and values, this depth and fervour*

about doing things well and striving for excellence, that comes closest to what I mean in describing a 'passionate teacher'.

Such teachers – and in sufficient numbers to constitute a critical mass of the staff complement – are clearly a prerequisite ingredient of the 'passionate school'.

Fried's words however deserve closer analysis because the first two sentences by implication are not definitions of the 'passionate teacher'. Yet they describe 'good' teachers, or certainly not bad teachers. What they do not possess is a sense of being driven by what they are doing – sometimes to the exclusion of almost all else – and a 'brooking-no-denial' or 'come-what-may' determination that those they teach will succeed, and that everyone they teach is unique and can access the same significant pleasure. They value those they teach and the pupils know it. This is what the remaining sentences of the Fried quotation imply as the feature of the passionate teacher.

'Passionate schools' might best be described as places where the critical mass of the school community enjoys a shared passion for learning in whatever sphere of activity motivates them plus a determination to excel both against their own previous personal best and be benchmarked against the highest standards of excellence from time to time. Moreover, they live and work in a community where they come together in teams or groups engaged in a shared activity in a passionate quest for collective excellence. Each member of the school community shows evident enjoyment in the prowess of other members and while there is competition among peers, it's a competitive edge that is tempered by the knowledge that they belong to a community which enjoys a magic of achievement shared by almost all. In summary, the members of a passionate school, and especially its many leaders, would relate to and find resonance in George Bernard Shaw's (2000) words for a character in *Man and Superman*:

This is the one true joy in life, the being used for a purpose recognised by yourself as a mighty one; the being a part of a great enterprise and a force of nature rather than a feverish, selfish little clod of ailments and grievances, complaining that the world will not devote itself to making you happy.

I am of the opinion that my life belongs to the whole community and that as long as I live it is my privilege to do for it whatever I can. I want to be thoroughly used up when I die for the harder I work, the more I live. I rejoice in life for its own sake. Life is no brief candle, to me it is a splendid torch which I have got hold of for the moment and I want it to burn as brightly as possible before handing it on to future generations.

This Shaw quotation conveys the meaning of 'passion' for all, whether it's the schoolteacher, the school pupil or the school leader we are describing.

Passionate teachers

The earlier Fried quotation specifically has the teacher in mind. The condition is best encapsulated for me by recalling two visits three years apart to Rhyn Park, a secondary school in a former mining community on the Shropshire border with Wales. My first visit to Rhyn Park was to present prizes at their awards evening some bleak February day in 1989. I had recently arrived as Professor in the Education faculty at Keele University. It was a long and tortuous drive and I arrived to find a headteacher and school community with their tails between their collective legs, for that very day the local paper branded the school 'the worst in Shropshire', as their five or more higher grades figure at 17 per cent was worse than any other Shropshire secondary school. The headteacher however was defiant and determined, and we proceeded through a long evening with a backdrop on stage of a highlighted figure of the 'super learner'. Each faculty or year leader said a few words as they introduced their chosen recipients of subject and other awards. Year 7 pupils sat wonderingly on a bench at the front. The evening closed at 10.30 and I stayed to talk with the head who was privately wondering if, not when, her efforts to transform the school culture would pay off. By the time I had driven home, it was well past midnight.

My second visit was three years later and followed a phone conversation when I took some persuading to repeat my role at their awards evening. 'But you must come' insisted the headteacher Janet Warwick, 'you'll find us a bit different'. So, against my better judgement I went knowing with a heavy heart that I was doubtless in for another long evening. And so I was, but what a difference. There was exactly the same format: the 'super learner' figure as a backdrop and the subject and year leaders presenting their award winners. On this occasion, however, the mood was so different. Everybody had their heads up – not down, and there was a constant buzz of fun and excitement in the hall. The tenor of the evening was exemplified by the head of maths whose speech, as he stood before the assembled throng of staff, governors, parents, pupils and dignitaries, went roughly as follows, 'Guess which school in the whole mighty county of Shropshire came first with 66 per cent of the age group gaining a higher grade GCSE?' He paused for dramatic effect. 'Church Stretton! And guess who was a miserable, pathetic second? We were. And … ' he swivelled to look at the headteacher accusingly, 'what did she do? Well you know what she's like … she said "Mr Smith, you get over to Church Stretton right away and find the explanation. We can't have Rhyn Park coming second." So I did, and discovered three possible solutions. The first I could dismiss straight away, namely the quality of the Head of Department. I suggested the second possibility to our Deputy Miss Voyles, but she said "Yes, they may prepare their lessons but I prepared my last in 1985 and if you think I am going to start again now, you have another think coming." And then I found the answer.' He paused for dramatic effect. 'The Church Stretton maths teachers are an average of half an inch taller than our department. Miss Black please stand up.' At which point a diminutive teacher on the front row got to her feet. 'Look at her. What can you say? Her chin is too close to her feet. But … ' He paused for dramatic effect. 'I have the answer. We appointed Mr Hudson last September. Mr Hudson is at the back.' Everyone turned to look at the new member of staff. 'He's six foot seven in his bare feet. I rest my case … next year Rhyn Park will be top of the maths league table.' He went on to cite the many winners of various categories culminating in the maths school prize for the subject given to a bemused girl who when I presented her prize, confessed she had no idea why she had received it as she was very good at art not maths. Mr Smith had overheard the exchange and told the audience, 'Judith wonders why she got the prize, well I'll tell you. She got a "C" as a result of enormous effort and I am telling you if Judith can get a "C" then everyone at Rhyn Park can and will get a "C" or better.'

At the conclusion of the proceedings I once again talked to the Head as I had done three years earlier. Her mood was changed too and when I asked her about the dramatic improvement – for the five or more higher grades figure was by then almost 60 per cent – she brought up Mr Smith, the mathematician, as an exemplar of the 'passion' that now permeated the staff. She had appointed him two years previously and he had chosen to teach the second bottom set and asked them how many expected to get a 'C', to which the answer was none and then how many would love to get a 'C', to which all confessed a private wish. So he had struck a bargain and proceeded to enthuse and explain so that they came on by leaps and bounds. He even took them on the occasional Sunday maths picnic, as part of his campaign to include all in his own love of numbers.

We agreed that Mr Smith was pretty unusual but for schools to be successful and passionate you needed a few members of staff like Mr Smith, people whose burning interest was contagious and acted as a liberating example to others to give full rein to their own particular enthusiasm. Although he used the imagery for a different purpose, Alec Clegg (1980) captured these enthusiasms in his description of the sampler on his aunt's living room wall:

> 'If of fortune thou be bereft
> And of thine earthly store have left
> Two loaves. Sell one and with the dole
> Buy hyacinths to feed the soul'

It's the finding and giving full rein to personal hyacinths, whether of staff or pupils in the school, that conveys at least some of what I mean by 'passion'.

Figure 1.1 sets out the beliefs, habits and behaviours of passionate and outstanding teachers.

They do not necessarily have all of these but they have most, allied perhaps to an obsession about what they are interested in, which is often though not always their subject, or which might be something as well as the subject they teach.

The list implies certain competencies which when allied to

Beliefs of passionate and outstanding teachers

- The transformability rather than the fixed or predictable ability of those they teach.
- Success is possible and expected for all pupils, and a failure to learn immediately is a challenge to their own teaching, not a sign of the pupil's inability to learn.
- Intelligence/talent is multifaceted rather than general and indicated by speed in problem solving, literacy and numeracy.
- A child showing great effort to learn is a sign of strong character, not of limited ability to learn.
- All the children they teach need a worthwhile relationship with at least one adult who may not be them.

Habits and behaviours of passionate and outstanding teachers

- Always reflect on and seek to improve their own story-telling techniques as a part of their skill in 'best explanations'.
- Store on DVD/learning platforms examples of their own and colleagues' best explanations for student use.
- Refine and extend their questioning skills and train their pupils in questioning for use in group work.
- Seek opportunities to teach/learn alongside and behind as well as in front of those they teach.
- Treat teaching and learning as a 'co-operative' activity, using 'we' a lot.
- Introduce their own 'hyacinths' of learning.
- Use formative and ipsative rather than normative assessment, especially in their marking of pupils' work.
- Talk about teaching and learning with their colleagues in faculty and staff meetings.
- Observe others' practice as well as seek video evidence of their own practice to inform their quest to improve.
- Teach in corridors and playgrounds.

Figure 1.1: *Beliefs, habits and behaviours of passionate and outstanding teachers*

passion are sure to bring success. The interrelationship of competence and passion necessary in the teacher and the school leader can be seen in Figure 1.2.

As we can see, the interaction of competence is crucial and the absence of both is a quick route to dysfunctional failure whether in the classroom or the school. Most schools will have some competence and some passion and will seek to build on both.

Nowhere is the combination of competence and passion more important than in the post of headteacher.

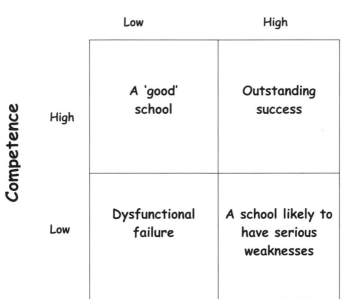

Figure 1.2: *Aligning passion and competence*

Passionate headteachers

Traditionally the connection between being a teacher and being a headteacher has been seen to be a necessary and essential requirement to command the respect of the community called 'school'. Look at the following 1930s description by Sir Michael Saddler of someone whom we can immediately recognize as a distinguished headteacher and it starts with his being a teacher (Clegg, 1980):

> *Samuel Clegg was an artist, a poet, a radical pioneer, a stringent, stimulating teacher, an undaunted soul … he had faith and character. His work in school was an intimate echo of his inner life. He loved his fellow men, gave himself generously for others and by losing himself in his appointed task, gained new life and power … Nothing but the best he believed was good enough for children and he strove to surround them with beautiful things and create for them*

*an environment that was charged with ... light. He believed that
education was much more than success in examinations, though a
long list of distinctions proved that the two were not incompatible.*

*He believed in the fundamental goodness of human nature, in
liberty, in gentleness and in the silent but inevitable influence of
cultivated surroundings ... He was a high voltage cable in a cordial and
progressive society [his school], a lover of beauty in literature, art
and landscape, an ardent believer in the capacity of almost all hearts
and minds to win, in Robert Bridge's words:*

New beauty of soul from the embrace of beauty
And strength by practical combat against folly and wrong.

Again there is the echo of the teacher's unshakeable belief in the
capacity of all to succeed. The identification of that and the roman-
ticism of the passage shouldn't obscure the need for the
competences which are presented as a matching matrix in Figure
1.3, especially in the modern world where schools are less insulated
from a society, where the pressures brought about by technologi-
cally driven and accelerated change demand a set of worldly-wise
characteristics from our school leaders. Nor should it hide the barriers that now exist for headteachers to remain the credible 'teaching'
leader of the school.

These barriers have arisen from the changes ushered in by the
1988 Education Act which both gave schools managerial control
and substantial powers of virement over their budgets and simultaneously relieved them of decisions about the curriculum which
became centrally prescribed in great detail. Matters affecting budgets and management formerly made by the local authority were
now for the school to decide. In the summer of 1993 in Birmingham
for example, headteachers regarded it as odd – albeit welcome – that
they were being asked to consider their educational leadership role
in school improvement. They knew that their counterparts elsewhere in the country were being encouraged to see themselves as
chief executives. It is easy to forget that for almost a decade after
1988, central government acted on the assumption that the introduction of the national curriculum and tests would take care of their
ambition to raise standards. Even when that misplaced belief shifted
to an emphasis on 'school improvement' and laid a heavy emphasis on the headteacher's responsibility in securing it, there remained

many obstacles to headteachers finding the time to assume the role of professional leader, especially if that involves, as it certainly does in a school with ambitions to be 'passionate', the headteacher providing an example by being seen to be involved in learning and teaching. One has only to see a few case study files of children with special educational needs or ask about the bureaucracy involved in 'police checks' of school personnel or consider the advice on 'performance management' to see how in an age of accountability, the role of the headteacher has become more demanding of managerial competence. It is extremely difficult therefore for the headteacher to find time for teaching and learning. Yet doing just that is one of the essential competences which the 'passionate leader' needs to demonstrate when carrying out six activities and tasks. I briefly examine these below.

Providing a credible example as learner and teacher

It is probably not sensible, as it once was, for the headteacher in the medium- or large-sized school to have a regular, timetabled teaching slot, even though this will of course be the case in the thousands of very small primary schools. The headteacher gets dragged away too frequently for that to be sensible, though many headteachers do take over when they have been unable to make a satisfactory appointment in the middle of the year. Passionate heads however find other ways to demonstrate their interest. For example they take over somebody's lessons every week for a half term in order to allow the teacher to make focused visits to other classrooms in their own or another school. This is part of a faculty, phase or whole-school quest to raise their individual and collective practice towards the elusive 'outstanding pedagogy' which is their ultimate goal. In doing so, not only do they release the teacher for a very persuasive form of professional development, they allow themselves to sample the standards in the classrooms where they are teaching so that discussions that follow can be grounded in a shared experience.

All 'passionate' headteachers know they have to be outstanding performers at assemblies and/or in going from class to class to talk persuasively to all the school about moral and often traumatic issues that have arisen as a result of international, national or local events. They see these as vital times to reassert values. Passionate leaders effortlessly engage with and respect the different expertise of their staff. So they share an article gleaned about maths from the *Times Educational Supplement* with the maths department and want their views as to its value. They will visit the art faculty meeting to learn of their opinion of a local exhibition and whether there's more that they could be doing in organizing the school to give full rein to the art faculty's ambitions for the pupils.

Above all, passionate leaders are always seen to be learning. Not only are they good at asking open ended as well as highly pointed questions, they are also skilled exponents of 'speculative remarks' – all designed to encourage the extension of their staff's reach to bring yet more within their grasp. They are what Michael Fullan has described as 'knowledge creators' often with research projects of their own.

Being an effective and inspiring storyteller and expert and enthusiastic questioner

Since classical times the ability of the passionate leader to be a storyteller has been well chronicled. In the recent past Hitler and Churchill provide contrasting examples of what might be called the 'skaldic' tradition best exemplified by Shakespeare's words for King Harry on the eve of Agincourt. The passion involved cannot be doubted but the context of warfare may not immediately appear appropriate for the school. 'Skald', however, is a Norwegian word for the eloquent poet who used to tell stories of past glorious successes to troops on the eve of or during the course of an expedition. Even though not the best image for school, it does evoke the need within the passionate school to tell and retell stories of the past, present and future achievements of different groups within the community. The headteacher is the lead storyteller and tends to cross reference any particular story to others which reflect on the shared values and differently brilliant actions of various members of the school community. An expert 'skaldic' headteacher links past to present and, speculatively, to future outstanding achievements, always talking about the achievements as slightly ahead of where they really are – not too far ahead of course as to be unbelievable. The art of the headteacher as storyteller encompasses imagery, metaphor, simile, analogy, allegory and an unerring sense of timing and occasion. As with the teacher, however, the competent leader is careful not to be the person who provides the answers even when invited to do so. More likely they respond with questions of their own which encourage the questioners to find the answers for themselves.

Mastering the advanced skills of delegation and encouraging 'risk takers'

It is easy to have casual conversations about delegation and in the process make assumptions which mask the subtleties of what is a skill that is particularly hard to master. Figure 1.3 sets out a list used in industrial management and training courses in the late 1980s.

1. Look into this problem. Give me all the facts. I will decide what to do.
2. Let me know the options with all the pros and cons of each. I will decide what to select.
3. Let me know the criteria for your recommendation, which alternatives you have identified and which one appears best to you with any risk identified. I will make the decision.
4. Recommend a course of action for my approval.
5. Let me know what you intend to do. Delay action until I approve.
6. Let me know what you intend to do. Do it unless I say not to.
7. Take action. Let me know what you did. Let me know how it turns out.
8. Take action. Communicate with me only if action is unsuccessful.
9. Take action. No further communication with me is necessary

Figure 1.3: *Mastering the advanced skills of delegation and encouraging 'risk takers'*

At a quick glance Figure 1.3 enables you to see the range of possible positions so far as delegation is concerned. Most of us would cheerfully admit to our 'default' setting, that is the position to which we naturally lean if we don't think consciously about where we should be on the spectrum in any given situation. Yet we know that to be half way competent we need to be at different points on the scale in different situations. Somebody new in a job for which they have prime responsibility will need you, as leader, to be prepared to be nearer the top – say at number five – rather than at number seven which a more experienced colleague undertaking a similar task might. The importance of the task and whether it involves more than one key member of staff, will affect the number ascribed to the nominated leader of the whole operation. Certainly, the effective, as opposed to the ineffective, passionate leader will avoid three behaviours in using the nine point delegation list. To be at the top on any occasion other than a matter of 'life and death crisis' would risk the passionate leader falling into the trap of being the dazzling heroic leader who disables others. To be at the bottom would fail to fan the embers of the enthusiasm or replenish the energy of someone entrusted with an unenviable task. Both the top and the bottom positions will not be places for the passionate leader to assume in exercising delegation. The third and worst mistake would be to start in one position, say seven, and then change your mind and not admit it by claiming you were at number five when something goes wrong. The passionate leader who is by definition strong in the affective domain, needs to remember that the first rule is to take the blame when it's not your fault and give the credit when something goes well rather than steal the limelight for oneself. This means that the passionate leader is likely to encourage some risk taking among staff who see their leader as less like the conductor of an orchestra but more like an accepted leader in a jazz ensemble where each member receives the applause and something is created on the hoof.

Creating capacity and energy among staff

The passionate headteacher leader has to have an almost infallible ability to select and then develop staff with similar passion. They are unlikely to make an appointment 'that will do because we didn't have a very good field', as one hapless and unfortunate headteacher remarked. Far more likely it will be a case of delaying despite pressing difficulties because, as one passionate and competent head put it, 'at interview we didn't find someone who would quite fit. We changed the timetable of what we taught for a year because we couldn't get a good enough person in design and technology'. Having been incredibly fussy about appointments and looking among candidates for some evidence of a consuming interest in the successful appointment, the competent headteacher then seeks out extra opportunities for any new appointment to feel special and to have opportunities to give full rein to their passion whether it is in their subject field or in some aspect of extra-curricular activity.

They know that they have to display a keen and convincing interest in parts of school life which are not their own 'hyacinth' – indeed for them the activity in question, for example sport or opera may be a 'loaf'. All however need encouragement and they know that the best form of encouragement is to be present and to ask open ended questions and to celebrate officially and in public the success of the rich tapestry of their school community's passions. They talk 'with' staff a lot and only 'about' staff to others to tell tales of great achievement. They spend the time the school is in session before and after school as well as during lesson time in walking from classroom to laboratory, from kitchen to offices to faculty rooms and staffroom, demonstrating their thirst for learning about each and every aspect of school life. Not for them a perceived preoccupation with the inevitable intractable problems – which they know are best dealt with as far as possible later and in private – but rather a restless interest in what's good and what's possible given their support.

They are experts in sharing. So they ensure all staff job descriptions enshrine shared leadership roles with 'prime' and 'support' responsibilities. Continuous professional development for them is a key and well resourced part of the school's annual budget as well as an integral part of any formalized 'appraisal' or 'performance management' system and they share their own with all staff. They set a personal example too in sharing by taking over someone else's job from time to time to enable the person released to engage on some visit to learn of other practice and by allowing others to chair important meetings. They create time-limited task groups of young and older members of staff to keep the tireless quest towards outstanding practice bubbling along by harnessing the intellectual curiosity and energy of everyone. Above all they never allow their own passion to cast an overwhelming shadow over the passions of others.

Seeking and charting improvement and constantly extending the vision

The wise headteacher knows that for a school to think that it has 'arrived' is a sure sign that they are dangerously poised to start a gradual decline. 'Outstanding' is the adjective most sought by UK schools today from the inspection of the Office for Standards in Education (OFSTED) but they realize to earn it brings with it all sorts of challenges. Will it be possible to sustain it and how do you avoid complacency? The passionate school simply accepts that 'outstanding' is a shifting horizon. How can you ever know that either the individual or the collective has ever reached the limit of what's possible? Learning without limits is part of their credo. So the passionate headteacher needs the competence to reinforce such a belief without adding to the exhaustion that is never far from members of the outstandingly successful school. A vital part of that is to impart to new members of the community a sense of 'legacy'. 'I take all the Year sevens each year' declared one headteacher, 'I explain to them the history of the school and the great deeds achieved by those who have been at the school before them, whether in sport, the arts, craft, practical and theoretical subjects – and I am careful to draw a distinction between those two aspects and stress they have equal value – or in service to others. I explain that in their turn they will contribute to that legacy. And I make sure the Heads of Year are always stressing how outstanding their year's pupils are and how proud the school will be of what they achieve. The general approach is re-enforced of course by the way that they and I at school assemblies celebrate the achievements of pupils as we go along.' Rather like the earlier story of Rhyn Park, her school awards days are times when a whole series and a wide range of human endeavour and success are rewarded. Another school ensured that part of its visual environment entailed the walls of the school hall being full of pen portraits of the achievements of past members of the school community as successful adults.

So a competence needed by the passionate headteacher is the

capacity to act as both a well informed guardian of the history of the school's past achievements and a futurologist with an uncanny knack of predicting the weather so that members of the community come to trust their view of what external factors are going to be important to the school. They only earn this latter trust by becoming sufficiently interested in all the passions that can form part of a school's life. The more the headteacher is able to ask searching questions about maths and science, history, geography and all the other humanity subjects, sport and the arts, modern languages and English and so on, the more likely it is that they can put together the interconnections of all aspects of school life with the external demands and form a good judgement about what lies ahead. Clearly the focus of such interest will vary from phase to phase. The headteacher of the primary school, where there are probably more examples of a school earning the soubriquet 'passionate', needs to show an interest in such matters at a different level from that necessary for the principal of a sixth form college. (One of the astonishing things I admired about the Vice-Chancellor at Keele University was his capacity to have worthwhile conversations with research leaders in each and every one of the many diverse disciplines that form the curriculum of that university.)

There is however no hiding from the necessity of using and encouraging the use of comparative collective data. It is possible to be passionate about data and other evidence: otherwise how can we be sure that we are using the right calibrations in our judgements about the value and worth of what is and what's not possible? So this competence of charting improvement involves encouraging the use of 'benchmarking', visits to other similar schools performing differently and the adoption of as many in the community as possible of a research theme affecting some aspect of their work.

Meeting and minimizing crisis and securing the environment

As anyone in school will know, crisis is never far from the surface of school life. Most frequently, factors external to the school precipitate its occurrence: an angry parent – or worse still, group of parents – , pupils who have brought into school some of the 'baggage' of challenged lives at home or in the community, staff who allow pressures to upset then from time to time or who are suddenly ill, a fatality among pupils or staff or their families.

Someone once said that the successful headteacher needed four qualities:

- regarding crisis as the norm, and complexity as fun;
- having unwarranted optimism;
- possessing an endless well of intellectual curiosity;
- having no sense of self-pity or paranoia.

Certainly this fourfold combination will enable the headteacher to meet and minimize crisis effectively. Yet it is too glib a definition for it begs the question of how a headteacher comes to have these qualities. Well they will certainly be skilled at being able to act as a 'utility player' by deploying their own albeit limited skills in an emergency, for example by teaching a subject in which their knowledge is tenuous, to cover at least briefly the temporary or longer-term absence of a key member of staff. It means too that they need to develop the capacity to hover over events while in the thick of them, rather as the Victorian factory owner, perched in a windowed office above the shop floor, could see the whole and yet in a moment – and frequently – come down their spiral staircase to be among the workers. This competence does not recognize the need for separate 'time to think' for they are thinking all the time.

At the heart of all these competences is the absolute requirement that there is integrity in the passionate leader. People need to see that there are no joins or gaps in what they are, what they say and what they do. And that brings us finally to values and the passionate school.

Passionate schools

In the conversations with the ten headteachers on which this chapter is based, all were agreed that 'values' were at the heart of a passionate and successful school and that although they were something they personally held strongly, they were also something that were shared across the school community. 'Why,' asked the headteacher who had taught legacy to Year 7 'do you think I go to all that trouble? It is because although we are buffeted by change, there are certain values which act as a moral compass for us all, including me.'

The headteachers involved expressed their sets of values with strikingly similar words. They would, I think, all subscribe with differing emphasis to the following two groupings.

Living one's life by the highest common factor from religious and humanist traditions

Notwithstanding the heated arguments that discussion of religions, of atheism and agnosticism involve, almost all schools rightly see it as their duty to provide an example for the young that highlights the importance of respecting truth, differences of opinion, of listening, of honest dealing and of treating others as you would yourself. Some would argue that it is easier for the faith school to promote these. After all they can pray in aid that part of the purpose of the school's foundation is expressly to ask for a shared subscription to such values. Certainly the headteachers of community schools will claim that it's harder for them to assert this particular set of shared values for human behaviour in an increasingly disputatious and contested world where, for example, some sections of the community will covertly resort to racism or see cheating the state as fair game. While that is true, it is also the case that faith schools frequently find the notion of pluralism as one that at least some members of their community find it hard to respect. Nevertheless this first shared value has to be present in the successful passionate schools otherwise the passion might come to be based on life values more akin to the Hitler Youth.

Striving for success for all pupils and staff rather than acting on the assumption that the reverse side of the success coin has to involve failure for some

All the headteachers were agreed that their own schooling had been unduly influenced by underlying professional assumptions of the need for failure. Many talked about frequent ranking of pupils in streamed classes and therefore an undue emphasis on competition between pupils. They were of a view that internal practices needed to reflect an expectation of success. Indeed one headteacher with whom I had shared the Rhyn Park story outlined earlier remarked:

I agree with your take on passion, passionate teachers, passionate headteachers, but I might be more pragmatic or utilitarian in that the inspirational teacher, the one beloved by politicians, the one who breaks the rules is wonderful but doesn't really help us much. What we need are teachers who are passionate about pupils getting five or more A–C including English and maths, or whatever else is their potential. The maths teacher you describe from Rhyn Park reminds me of our head of maths. He is a good but not inspirational class-room teacher, but he is absolutely driven when it comes to pupil attainment. He knows every pupil in Year 11 and Year 9 for that matter; exactly where they are with their coursework and what they will have to do to reach or exceed their targeted grade. He does before-school classes, Saturday classes, holiday classes, coursework catch-up, etc. He has also had to deal with high staff turnover and very inexperienced teachers over the last ten years, yet he manages to hold it all together and achieve excellent results because he is pas-sionate about the pupils succeeding.

That's not to say that the rest of the school don't care about the quality of teaching and learning. We have put a huge effort over the last few years into trying to improve that but in the end the reason we have had the success we have in raising attainment is because of the collective commitment to core values about individual pupils' success. On exam results day in August, we frequently have 30 plus teachers and support staff coming in and many more telephoning because, despite our commitment to a broad and balanced education and all the other extra curricular stuff which is so important, for our pupils and those in similar circumstances, the exam results are more important if they want to have any chance of competing for the opportunities that are out there.

This provides a vivid reminder of the need for an overriding passion for pupils' success which is so much more than a romantic 'Dead Poets' Society' view of what passionate teachers and passionate schools do. Another headteacher who believes that if you fan the passions of sport, art, drama, music and outdoor pursuits, 'it is almost certain that you will strike a rich vein in almost all your pupils', would also agree the overriding importance of the staff being passionate about the pupils' ultimate success.

What's clear moreover is that both headteachers act out on a daily basis their passionate belief that all pupils can succeed in some area that will equip them for a fulfilling life. In short, they see talent as multi-faceted and therefore that their schools will be more inclusive places.

Although my sample of ten headteachers were with one exception drawn from the secondary sector, it's worth speculating whether passionate schools are more likely to be found in the primary sector. It is at least arguable that childhood offers more hope and less distracting complexity than adolescence when among other things there are more inhibitions and frequently the need on the part of the pupil to be an instant expert and not to look a fool in front of their peer group. And I guess therefore the passion that matters – the belief that all can and will succeed – is the easier to create among more staff. Nevertheless, both in special schools and particularly inner city and challenged secondary schools, there is increasing evidence that headteachers are much less accepting that there need to be limits on what they can achieve. Not for them the reluctant acceptance that the formidable circumstances some pupils face beyond the school mean their efforts will come to naught. They prefer to see them as challenges to extend that combination of passion and skill that will 'unlock the mind and open the shut chambers of the heart'.

References

Clegg, A. (1980) *Around our Schools*. Oxford: Blackwell.

Fried, R. (2002) *The Passionate Teacher: A Practical Guide*. Boston, MA: Beacon Press.

Shaw, G. B. (1903) *Man and Superman*. London: Penguin.

Passionate leadership

Chapter 2

Inviting passionate educational leadership

John M. Novak

What are dedicated and discerning educational leaders to do? On the one hand, at an ideal level, they realize that education is a deeply meaningful activity that involves high degrees of intensity and commitment. Without this intensity and commitment educators run the risk of merely going through the motions until the final bell rings, an image that conjures up being frozen in Dante's lowest level of hell. On the other hand, in their daily professional lives, often, way too often, they see the pompous posturing of a pseudo-passionate personality promoting goods of questionable value. Passionate new people continually come into positions of high level leadership selling the latest, the greatest, programme or policy with the aim to boost their own narrow vocational ambitions. They seem to be 'faking it until they make it' and then will be gone to their next step up the success ladder before anything of significance is done. Are an educational leader's hands tied? Is it a choice between unthinking but dedicated passion or critical but disengaged discernment? Certainly educators should not promote either unthinking or disengagement. Just as John Dewey (1938) warned of the danger of thinking in terms of distorting either/ors, there are other more creative and life-affirming choices that can be constructed. This chapter will present an inviting approach to educational leadership that seeks to call forth passion and discernment. Based on the idea that it is essential for educational leaders to care about passion and be passionate about caring, passionate leadership will be explored.

Passionate educators are not to be denied, but they may need to be advised. Several years ago one of my colleagues described how she was working with a group of energetic educators who wanted to keep doing more and more, with ever-higher levels of enthusiasm. They had before-school programmes, after-school programmes, weekend programmes, and programmes about programmes. While she admired their passion, she pointed out that it looked as if they were burning the candle from both ends. Praising their efforts, she asked them what they wanted from her. They said, 'More wax!' These educators were seeking, they were strong, and they wanted to be in it with their whole heart. However, without a guiding educational vision and creative strategies, their passion would be gone and soon they would be frustrated, exhausted, and join the ranks of the burned out. This chapter is also about the examination, production and deployment of the passionate leadership needed to keep the educational candles lit.

Being an educational leader is not for the faint of heart or those who want to feign a heart. It is not for those who do not want to be fired up or who are deathly afraid of being fired. Ultimately it requires people who are in it for the long run, who seek not merely to survive, not merely to personally succeed, but sincerely desire to be an important part of a highly valued endeavour. If education can be viewed as fundamentally an imaginative act of hope (Novak, 2002), passionate educational leadership is about calling forth and sustaining the conditions that encourage the persistence, resourcefulness and courage necessary to provide the wax, the substance, to keep the flame lit. Although this is easier said than done, this chapter will also look at inviting passionate educational leadership and provide a guide for sustaining it for the long run. With this in mind, it will be argued that passion needs to be connected to care if it is to endure; leadership needs to listen if it is going to expand; education needs to deepen experience, if it is to matter; and inviting needs to be a creative *modus operandi* if flames are going to glow and grow.

Caring to explore passionate leadership

We live in a contradictory age, an age of ease and tension, of freedom and control, where people both seek deep passion and are deeply suspicious of it. To some, passionate leadership is a good thing to be sought regardless of the price. To others, it is a danger to be avoided because the squeaking goose gets shot. To a cynical few, it is an oxymoron to be scoffed because it cannot be sustained in the management jungle. At the very least, it is a concept that needs to be explored. Exploring a concept can unpack some of the assumptions embedded in our often unreflected experiences and take us to a more nuanced level of understanding. This exploration can be done by looking at five myths of passionate leadership.

Myth 1: Passionate leadership is a good thing. It certainly can be a good thing if a leader is passionate about the right things for the right reasons in the right ways, but obviously that is not always the case. This means that passionate leadership, to be worthwhile, needs to be connected with a coherent approach for dealing with people in ethical ways. To paraphrase Immanuel Kant: Passionate leadership without ethics is blind. Ethics without passionate leadership is empty. The merging of a deep sense of caring with that which has profound educational worth is the artistic expression of a thoughtful sense of passionate educational leadership.

Myth 2: Passionate leadership is necessary to motivate people. This assumes that people need to be motivated by an external source if they are going to be active. However, if it is assumed that people are already motivated, as some theorists propose (Kelly, 1963, Combs, 1982, Purkey and Novak, 1996, Purkey, 2000, Novak, 2002), then external attempts to motivate are misdirected at best and manipulative at worst. Working with the idea that people already possess internal motives that are to be worked with leads to qualitatively different ways to relate. This assumption of an ongoing internal motive leads to a person-oriented ethics of doing-with relationships rather than a manipulative style of doing-to domination. A doing-with sense of ethics comports well with the ideals of a democratic society.

Myth 3: Passionate leadership involves an unwarranted optimism. Although it may appear this way to people who possess the view that the default position of everyday life is a warranted pessimism, there are other alternatives. The idea of a warranted meliorism, where bad things might be made less bad and good things might be made better, is based on a view of positive psychology (Seligman,

2002) that has solid empirical support. This pragmatically hopeful melioristic perspective is centred on having an 'orientation of open, attentive readiness to possibilities of satisfaction' (Shade, 2001: 20) along with a critical, creative and persistent penchant to make things better. From this melioristic perspective, better things have a better chance of happening when it is assumed that positive outcomes are possible but not guaranteed. This is a warranted approach that depends on a personal and professional leadership stance that tries to move in a positive direction and grows through self-correcting enquiry.

Myth 4: Passionate leadership is based on an authentic sense of certainty. At first this seems true by definition. If the word passion implies the willingness to suffer for a cause, feeling strongly that you are doing the right thing would seem essential. It certainly would seem easier to be passionate about something if you have no doubts about it. However, in our so-called postmodern age, where reality isn't what it used to be and metanarratives of certainty are certainly questioned (Anderson, 1990), the passion of certainty has vacated the premises for many who engage in deliberative discussions with those of differing positions (Mutz, 2006). It is not easy to be certain when those you like and respect have very different views. Also, the idea that you may have to 'fake it until you make it' implies that certainty may have to be tried on before it can take hold. Cognition may be ahead of affect and the head may have to develop strategies to get the heart up-to-speed. In cases where sincere feelings may not take hold, certainty may only be a strategic posturing necessary to obtain or retain power (Crawford, 2007). From the perspective of the appearance of power, passionate pretence works better than caring caution. The quest for certainty, as John Dewey (1929) passionately and discerningly noted in his book with that title, can keep us caged in simplistic slogans and degenerative practices. Certainty can be the enemy of freedom and the force that stops needed discussion.

Myth 5: Passionate leadership begins with a positive attraction to something seen as good. The first definitions of 'passionate' in my dictionary are as follows: '1a: easily aroused to anger b: filled with anger: ANGRY' (*Merriam-Webster's Collegiate Dictionary*, 1993: 849). This is not the definition of a happy emotion of content but a negative reaction of dissatisfaction. Although a passionate approach may come about in many ways, it seems to get its edginess from rebellion. As Albert Camus (1956) noted in his book, *The Rebel*, a rebel is someone who is saying 'NO' because a 'YES' is not being actualized. We are shaken out of our contented state by something that is wrong, something that should not be happening. Seeking the 'YES' behind the 'NO' is vital for cutting with the positive edge of growth (Ury, 2007). Passionate leadership needs to acknowledge both its affirmative and negative sides if it is to keep its attraction and edge.

To summarize, caring about passionate leadership means to recognize its positive and negative qualities; to see that it is often built on a manipulative form of motivation; to understand that it can, with some effort, be grounded in a warranted meliorism; to realize that the expression of certainty can be inauthentic or unnecessary; and to acknowledge that beginning with the negative can be a way of moving to the larger positive. Let's now look more closely at a basic and deepening view of leadership that builds on a more caring understanding of passionate possibilities for a more democratic world.

Leadership that is passionate about caring

There is a new, more deeply involving sense of leadership that is struggling to be born. Understanding what it is up against, and has to work with, may facilitate the birthing process.

A traditionally accepted view of passionate leadership is that it implies someone (often, but not always, a man) with a vision (a clear, or an attractively vague picture of what must be), who can articulate that vision (usually, but not always, in a strong, indubitable tone), and enrol others (of lesser intensity and commitment) in that vision. Vision, articulation and enrolment of participants are key formal dimensions. However, even if we accept these formal dimensions, the gender, epistemological and hierarchical assumptions need to be challenged in an ethical approach to passionate leadership based on more democratic educational relationships.

In a deeply pluralistic world where gender domination is seen as morally reprehensible, the loud, booming, unwavering voice of the victorious patriarch is often viewed with suspicion and scorn. Vision, if it is to be ethical and effective in dealing with a highly complex, potentially democratic world, needs to be informed by the variety of voices trying to make sense of their individual and collective lives. This new emerging communicative vision of passionate leadership sees the necessity of people listening to each other to find meaningful things to hold in common so a deeper sense of community develops. This deeper sense of community, if it is to be ethically and democratically sensitive, needs to pay attention to the voices that have been traditionally marginalized in the larger societal and smaller local conversations.

In terms of the second formal characteristic, articulation of a vision is still important for a new type of passionate leader. Being able to put possibilities into words is an important skill. But it also can be much more than a skill; it can also be an aesthetic sensibility to more imaginative ways to be in the world. Imagination, as John Dewey (1934) noted, is the chief instrument of the good. A social aesthetic sensibility involves a feeling about how others perceive what is happening and what is imaginatively possible. As an important instrument of the good, a social aesthetic sensibility enables a leader to articulate a developing vision of what is desirable and makes sense to an emerging community. This moves articulation well beyond cognitive and rational skills to work with the deepest aspirations and hopes of people. The imaginative new passionate leadership involves more than one person, the person in charge, feeling others' pain and possibilities. It encourages all involved to be active participants, using this social aesthetic sensibility to deepen and create with the felt qualities mutually experienced. Like a good jazz band, a common theme is expressed and imaginative new directions are explored and continued.

Moving to the third characteristic, leaders without followers may be articulate visionaries in the abstract but unless others join them, they are merely auto-didactic icons in the concrete. Passionate leaders are more apt to enrol participants if those participants are able to enjoy the process. Enjoyment can come from a sense of flow (Csikszentmihalyi, 1997) in which activities are challenging but not overly threatening. This new view of passionate leadership involves the aesthetic skill of helping to structure work so as not to be overwhelming (stress stretching), or underwhelming (boredom breeding). Easier said than done, especially with pluralistic groups with differing histories and interests, passionate leaders who seek to reach 'aha!' moments with their groups, often use ha-ha experiences. Humour, sensitively used, can get a group to handle difficult issues in insightful ways and develop a deeper sense of connection, of we-ness, with others.

To summarize, this emerging view of passionate leadership emphasizes visions that listen to a variety of voices; articulation that builds on aesthetic sensibilities; and enrols participants who can enjoy the process. This new view of passionate leadership is highly democratic and can be better articulated if its vision of education is explored.

Education that deepens experience

The passionate educational leadership that is being promoted here is different from business leadership, more than school leadership, and goes well beyond philosophical leadership (Novak, 2002). It is different from business leadership because its primary motive is not to make money but to call forth and develop human potential. It is more than school leadership because a school is only one source, albeit an important source, of educational experiences. It goes well beyond philosophical leadership because it not only seeks to be clear about a vision, it attempts to bring that vision to life and life to that vision.

Education is the heart of the passionate leadership described here because it answers the question: 'Passionate about what?' Quite simply, as a result of being more educated a person should be able to appreciate more of his or her individual and collective experiences. 'Appreciating' is a key word and has three meanings that are vital to educative experiences: savouring (to recognize with gratitude), understanding (to grasp the nature of), and bettering (to increase the value of). Leaders who are passionate about education want others and themselves to lead more educational lives by appreciating more of life's potential. Let's explore this possibility.

Savouring is an important part of an educational experience. In an aesthetic sense it involves the quality of the connection that develops between a person and the activity he or she is involved in.

It is the authentic feeling of being in the present and appreciating the presence of what is happening. In promoting savouring, an educator is inviting people to live wide-awake and participate meaningfully with the ongoing events around. Savouring is a way of saying no to a fast-food world where people are consuming more and more, faster and faster, and enjoying it less and less. Savouring is saying yes to the cultivation of enjoyment and can be seen in such organizations as the Slow Food movement (Petrini, 2003). It is a way of enjoying the process. Passion needs savouring if it is to have a solid grounding. The desire and ability to take in more of the world, others and ourselves in a sensitive and thoughtful way provides the fuel to work against that which continually pushes us to move at more frenetic, future-oriented paces. For passionate educational leaders to call forth savouring in others, they must enjoy and model a savouring way of life themselves. To expect savouring for others but not oneself is to be viewed as suspect, as someone who reads recipes but does not know how to cook.

While savouring provides an aesthetic appreciation of the world, understanding is about the quality of the cognitive connection. Taken literally, to understand is to stand under and see how things come together. To grow in understanding is to be able to sort out the world in more meaningful ways, to see structures, connections and opportunities not previously envisioned. An educational leader focusing on understanding is saying no to that which confuses, distorts and trivializes, while saying yes to disciplined enquiry (Gardner, 1999) and thinking with exciting ideas that connect to real experiences, what Perkins (1992) calls a 'hot cognitive economy'. To say yes to understanding is to affirm complex cognitive events, to seek to make more subtle differentiations in experience, and to construct an evolving integrative framework for grasping greater possibilities and appreciations.

Education is not only about aesthetics and cognition, it is about ethics, caring to make the world a better place, a place where more people can have more opportunities to savour, understand, and improve their experiences. From the point of view of the emerging passionate approach to leadership emphasized here, bettering human experiences means enabling more and more people to be included in what Richard Rorty (1989) calls our 'we intentions'. It is saying no to cruelty and indifference and saying yes to the horizontal progression of feelings of empathy and compassion. It is about expanding the circle of human solidarity (Singer, 2002).

To summarize, leaders who are passionate about education take care to call forth activities that promote the savouring, understanding and bettering of collective and individual experiences. They are passionate about inviting educational living in others and themselves.

An inviting approach to passionate leadership

For passionate leadership to be desirable, it must be about the right thing for the right reason and be manifested in the right way. Otherwise it is too dangerous, self-serving, or unreliable. The position that has been presented here is that passionate leadership should be about the promotion of educational living because this will enable more and more people to live with a deeper sense of aesthetic, cognitive and moral appreciation. This ideal presentation of educational purpose and justification needs a method, a framework for implementation, or else it runs the risk of being so high minded that no one can oppose it but also being so far out of reach that no one can really practice it. What is needed is a good way to put into practice the ideals of an approach to passionate educational leadership that is defensible and desirable.

Previously it was noted that passion needs to be connected to care if it is to take hold; leadership needs to listen if it is going to democratically expand; and education needs to deepen experience, if it is to matter. This section will argue that an inviting approach needs to be a creative *modus operandi* if passionate flames are going to glow and grow.

From the point of view of an inviting passionate perspective for leadership, education can be seen as fundamentally an imaginative act of hope. Hope here is an active virtue that involves persistence, resourcefulness and courage (Shade, 2001). This hope can be manifested in a communicative approach to the educative process that has three touchstones: the heart, head, and hands. Touching the heart means that it should connect with an educator's deepest intuitions; touching the head means that it should make good sense; touching the hands means that it should lead to sound and creative practices.

The inviting approach to education attempts to integrate a leader's feelings, thoughts and actions. It is based on the observation that people are living in message environments that continually inform them of their worth, ability and conscientiousness. From birth to death people are receiving, interpreting and acting upon verbal, nonverbal, formal and informal messages that either call forth or shun their potential. These messages are communicated through people, places, policies, programmes and processes. It is the passionate concern of inviting educational leaders to promote affirmative message environments, and work to put an end to signals and systems that demean positive human possibilities. This heartfelt commitment has led to the development of an inviting theory of practice and the Inviting School movement. The rest of this chapter will look at an inviting theory of practice and its connection with passionate leadership.

Principles for an inviting theory of practice

A theory of practice is a self-correcting way of thinking about what is worthwhile doing. An invitational theory of practice is an interconnected set of principles, foundations, concepts, insights and strategies that works from the framework of developing doing-with relationships. Quite succinctly, the inviting theory of education is a democratically oriented, perceptually anchored, self-concept approach to the educative process that centres on the following five interlinking principles.

1. People are valuable, able and responsible and should be treated accordingly.
2. The process of educating should be a collaborative, cooperative activity.
3. The process, the way we go about doing something, is the product in the making.
4. All people possess untapped potential in all areas of worthwhile human endeavour.
5. This potential can be realized by places, policies, programmes and processes designed to invite development, and by people who are intentionally inviting with themselves and others personally and professionally.

These five principles both focus and constrain an invitational leader's passionate commitments. The first principle commits educators to develop ethical practices that call upon participants to take ownership of their learning and commitments. The second principle is a commitment to a doing-with process in which all participants are 'in it together'. Education is a communicative activity that works best when everyone is a participant in the process. Moving to the third principle, because ends and means cannot be separated, how you do something influences what you end up with. To do unethical things for good reasons has negative consequences that live on. The fourth principle asserts that all of us are only using a small part of our individual and collective potential. We all can grow, whether we realize it or not. Finally, the fifth principle takes seriously the idea that we are never neutral in our dealings with others. Everything we do and every way we do things either adds to or subtracts from the process of being a beneficial presence. With that being the case, it is important to be cognizant about and intentional in sending messages that call forth human development. The passion needed to put flesh on the bones of these principles is deepened by a grasp of the theoretical foundations of the inviting theory of educational practice.

Foundations for inviting passionate leadership

The inviting approach is a product of and a contributor to the democratic ethos, perceptual tradition and self-concept theory. Together these interlocking foundations emphasize the significance of each person and his or her world view and internal sense of motivation. Without a solid foundation, passionate invitational leadership runs the risk of being perceived as just another blast of hot air. Let's first turn to democracy.

Often democracy is a word thrown around by people on opposing sides of an issue. Claiming your opponent is undemocratic is a strong accusation used by people of various political stripes to gain an edge in the struggle for power. Moving beyond accusation and political strategy, the democratic ethos is an ideal that simply states that everyone matters. As an ideal, this simple statement expresses a commitment to treating people as ends not means and to acknowledging their integrity and personhood by facilitating their right to participate in decisions that affect them. This democratic ideal provides direction and constraints in working with people, leaving the specifics to be deliberated in particular situations. If ideals are seen as pragmatic guides, the democratic ethos should not be viewed as an ultimate goal that must be attained once and for all but rather as something that points us in a desirable direction and enables us to be more of what we want to become. Ideals are tools to direct our growth and are sharpened as they are put into practice.

If we take seriously the democratic ideal that everyone matters, then how particular individuals see things matters. The perceptual tradition looks at the world from the vantage point of an individual, seeing the world from the inside out. Rather than viewing people as bubbling cauldrons seeking release (Freudian psychology), or ping-pong balls with memory (Behaviourism), or information processing machines dealing with 0s and 1s (Cognitivism), the perceptual tradition deals with the interpretations that individuals make of events and themselves. These interpretations are the psychological reality for each person and when ignored or manipulated, make a person an object and not a psychological or moral subject. An appreciation of the perceptual tradition is vital in helping develop the empathy and imagination needed for holding things in common and developing a sense of community.

Following from the perceptual tradition, self-concept theory emphasizes how people view who they are and how they fit into the world. All perceptions are not primarily about self, but the focusing of the self is a component, to some degree, of all perceptions. Everyone's self perception helps focus other perceptions and, importantly, works to maintain, protect and enhance the present self system. From this point of view, there is no such thing as an unmotivated person. Although people may not do what we want them to do, they are motivated to keep their present self system going. Working with people in doing-with relationships means that it is not necessary to turn on their engine because it is always running. Better energy is expended in paving the road. Of particular importance for educational leaders is self-concept-as-learner. In a more educative world, learning to continuously learn is a central concern. Inviting people to see themselves as valuable, able and responsible learners is a way to help construct such a world.

In summary, the three interlocking foundations emphasize the ethical ideal of the worth of each person, the psychological and ethical importance of attending to the interpretations individuals make, and the motivational significance of thinking in terms of self-system maintenance, protection and enhancement. These foundations, along with the previously mentioned assumptions enable an educator to passionately reject disinviting behaviours and to enthusiastically say yes to intentionally inviting behaviours.

Inviting and disinviting ways of being

If we live in message environments that either call forth or shun human potential, it is important for educators to be aware of the directions and intent of the messages being sent and received. There are many ways to organize an understanding of these messages. However, a simple four-level classification (disinviting/inviting; unintentional/intentional) calls attention to important characteristics.

Intentionally disinviting messages aim at taking the heart out of others by communicating to them that they are essentially incapable, worthless, or irresponsible. When I get people to talk about intentionally disinviting messages they received in school, even many years ago, they display keen memories of the incidents along with visible anger and hurt. One of my students, a 55-year-old teacher, said her first grade teacher angrily told her that she was a stupid little girl who would never read well. My student said that she really never saw herself as a good reader and she was not going to blame the teacher for that. She did say, though, that the teacher had no right to say what she said and that in her own teaching she worked really hard not to use put-downs on her students. Passionate invitational educational leaders are justifiably upset by intentionally disinviting messages, do not justify them, and work to understand the people and contexts in which they occur so that changes can be made.

Unintentionally disinviting messages are sent by people 'who know not what they do'. These educators may be insensitive, abrupt and clueless about the effects their behaviours have on others. Probably the greatest number of disinviting messages are unintentional. Although these messages are not intended to harm, they are still felt strongly by those affected. One of the classic unintentionally dis-inviting messages is the phrase: 'It's easy, you can do it'. Although this might not be seen as negative to many people, to some it is a very threatening statement. What if you cannot do something that's easy? What does that make you? Passionate invitational leaders create settings where people can talk about the messages they receive and how they interpret them. Discussions about interpretations of messages can be a way to promote growth through creative tension.

Unintentionally inviting educators are the natural tail-waggers who have stumbled on to some good-natured ways of doing things but cannot explain why they work. Although on the surface this seems like a good thing, being unreflective causes difficulties when their usual ways of doing things are no longer working. Being out of touch, people at this unintentional level have a tendency to revert to lower levels, putting their foot in their mouth, or getting angry when situations change. Flying by the seat of one's pants is not good enough for navigating in our rapidly changing world.

Intentionally inviting is the highest level because actions are both positive and thought out. At this level a leader is able to maintain thoughtful passion, resourceful persistence and creative personality in the messages sent. Being reflective, intentionally inviting leaders can give defensible reasons for what they do, consider alternatives and exhibit a high degree of educational integrity. Passionate inviting leaders are committed to being intentionally inviting, even in the most difficult situations. They work at developing a deeper aesthetic sensibility that gives them more imaginative ways to be proactive, to getting the ball rolling.

Passion and the Five Ps

Being intentionally inviting is brought to life in the creative ways people focus the energies of their personalities, places, policies, programmes and processes. Each of these five areas of focus can be approached with a subtle and sustained passion that creates an aesthetically harmonized whole. Let's turn first to people.

Invitational leadership begins and ends with people. Passionate invitational leaders know that since nobody is neutral, everyone within the school is an emissary of the school. How people relate to each other matters and what is sought is a deep-seated collegiality, not a contrived congeniality. This collegiality is manifested in the respect given for each person's competence and commitment to making the school a good place for everyone to be.

It is hard to hide from places. They tend to be everywhere. The appearance and upkeep of a school sends a message about the care, competence and commitment of the people who are there. Passionate invitational leaders have a dedication to making the signs in their school user friendly. One principal I worked with said that the State of Delaware required him to have posted the disinviting sign, 'Visitors must report to the office', at the entrance of his school. He complied, but on top of that sign he had one posted that said, 'Welcome to our school. In order for us to better help you and for the safety of our students, would you please report to the office which is 50 feet to the right'. In brackets a little lower, he had the additional message, 'The State of Delaware has not learned about inviting signs yet and the law requires that we have to have the sign below officially posted'. What a powerful message his sign sent. He found a way to obey the law, add a little humour and convey a passionate message about his school. He was passionate about the idea that there is always something that could be done.

The policies of a school are its written and unwritten rules and codes of conduct. A school with passionate invitational leadership displays its mission statement not only in words, but also in the inclusive, democratic, and respectful ways in which these words were developed and how they will be evaluated. A specific policy that can have a surprisingly powerful effect is the way the telephone is answered at the school. Quite simply, the person answering the phone should provide a greeting, identification and offer of assistance. In a workshop with some 50 principals who wanted to develop a more inviting school, I asked them to call their school and give one dollar to charity if all three aspects were not stated. More than 40 dollars was given to charity that day.

The programmes of a school are the heart of its social, intellectual and cultural being. Formal and informal curricular and co-curricular activities that are perceived as racist, sexist, elitist or homophobic communicate very disinviting messages. A curriculum that lacks intellectual integrity sends a message that depth and disciplined enquiry do not matter. Passionate invitational leaders care about what is taught and learned in schools. This goes well beyond raising standardized test scores. In addition, intentionally inviting educational leaders have in-school and out-of-school activities to take insiders out of the school and bring outsiders into the school.

Processes deal with the old adage, 'It don't mean a thing, if you ain't got that swing'. How the previous four Ps are harmonized into an inviting whole sends a message about the aesthetic sensibilities of the school. In orchestrating the Five Ps, the Processes Team orchestrates the other four Ps. Done with aesthetic passion, this is communicated with the strong sense that this is our school and we are all in it together. The members of this orchestrating Process Team have caught the inviting spirit and are passing it on to all they come in contact with. Inviting passionate leadership aims to be contagious. For this to happen, it also has to be nurtured.

Sustaining inviting passionate leadership

Passionate invitational leaders expect a lot from themselves and others. It is much easier to have low expectations and be occasionally surprised than to have high expectations and be vulnerable. But nobody said that inviting passionate educational leadership is easy, only that it is worthwhile. Persistence, resourcefulness and courage need to be nurtured in order to maintain, protect and enhance the passion to be in it for the long run. When I introduce people to the inviting approach, I am often asked, 'How long should I be inviting?' Sometimes people even get Biblical and say 'Seven times? 70 times? 70 times 70 times?' Rather than go along with this quantitative line of reasoning, I tell people that they should invite as long as their heart can endure. In order to be a hearty inviter, it is necessary to invite oneself and others personally and professionally. Each of these dimensions needs attention and is part of an integrated whole.

Inviting oneself personally affirms the importance of living an educational life oneself. If inviting educational leaders are going to summon all others to live fulfilling lives, they should show that they are responding to their own summons. Passionate educational leadership will not survive if it is based on continual self-sacrifice, which is a recipe for resentment, withdrawal and regressive behaviour. Inviting oneself personally is about savouring, understanding and making improvements in one's own life. A particular inviting challenge is to seek some 'personal firsts', some new activities that will enrich one's life. In addition, paying attention to one's self talk, the things we say to ourselves in the privacy of our own mind, is a good personal place to demonstrate intentionally inviting practices. Finding ways to construct realistic and positive assessments of situations and oneself is a way to develop and strengthen one's sense of personal hope.

Inviting others personally means acknowledging that life gains meaning when it is shared with others who care. In an intentionally inviting school, the social committee has a special responsibility to keep the spark alive and communicate the feeling that we are all in this together. Acknowledging people's birthdays and other special events in their lives brings a school closer together. One superintendent of schools sent a note to the parents of one of his principals telling them what a good job their son was doing. Their son, the principal, said he saw the note stuck on the refrigerator with a magnet. His parents were so proud of him and he was so impressed with his superintendent that he got over his initial embarrassment.

Inviting oneself professionally means to read, write and confer to stay alive intellectually, emotionally and socially. These are interesting times to be alive. As the world is becoming more connected and complex, ingenuity is required to anticipate what is going to happen and to slow aspects of our already too-rushed lives (Homer-Dixon, 2000). Passionate invitational leaders are concerned with the world outside the school and see how that world impinges on the school and in what ways the school impinges on the world. Writing for professional publication is a way to more deeply connect with the world outside the school. Having in-school forums is a way to connect the outside world with the school.

Inviting passionate educational leadership is about intentionally inviting others professionally. It is about helping others develop a strong self-concept-as-learner so they can relate, assert, invest and cope with making sense of the world of knowledge (academic disciplines) and the world for knowledge (the world at large that makes available patterns, challenges and mysteries). Inviting others to relate is to ask them to trustingly connect with others and the human condition; inviting others to assert is to ask them to develop a sense of integrity to speak up and claim their voice; inviting others to invest is to ask them to identify with more people and parts of life by trying new activities; inviting others to cope is to ask them to deal competently and caringly with life's demands and possibilities. To repeat, this is not for the faint of heart or those who do not want to be fired up by the aesthetic, cognitive and moral challenges and opportunities of educational living.

Beyond the myths of inviting passionate educational leadership

Just as the idea of passionate leadership needed to be looked at more deeply to get a better sense of its possibilities, so too does inviting passionate educational leadership need to be explored. Myths and shallow thinking about inviting passionate leadership can lead to cynicism, foolishness and neglect. Here are five myths that need to be transcended if inviting passionate educational leadership is to be better understood and sustained.

Myth 1: Inviting passionate educational leadership means you have to be perfect. Perfection, in many ways is a variant of 'the best'. Both words can get in the way of the better. Inviting passionate educational leadership is for mere mortals and is based on a self-correcting theory of practice. In trying to be an inviting leader, a person is simultaneously a practitioner, theorist and researcher. That means that when something does not work you go back to the drawing board and think through the way of thinking and acting in a specific situation and examine the consequences that ensued. This thinking, doing and further reflecting deepens the inviting theory of practice.

Myth 2: People have to be 'on' all the time to be passionate inviting educational leaders. People who are 'on' all the time will burn the candle from too many sides and will run out of wax. Being 'on' has its time and place but it can be unintentionally disinviting if it is artificial and the only side shown of one's personality. If we invite others personally we have a solid support group who are on our side personally and who appreciate who we are now and encourage the development of our better self. This means an inviting educational leader has to accept as well as extend invitations.

Myth 3: Inviting passionate invitational leadership is too simple. It is true that the inviting approach is based on the simple idea that if we are living in a world of messages, then we can intentionally construct messages that seek to call forth positive human possibilities. Although this is a simple idea, it is not always easy to implement in a world of growing complexity. A simple idea does not mean an easy idea, and needs to be distinguished from a simplistic idea, one that makes a caricature of an event. Done well, a simple idea captures the essence of something and provides a handle on complexity. A simplistic idea, by contrast, blocks connections to more nuanced understandings and possibilities and unintentionally makes things much more complicated and much more troublesome.

Myth 4: Inviting passionate educational leadership requires a certain specified way of doing things. The inviting approach has a perceptual base, which means that it acknowledges that there are many innumerable ways to view and do things that matter. From this point of view, a person does not have to follow a pre-arranged script but works to develop and use the signature strengths of his or her personality. It is the art of using one's personality as an instrument that gives life and originality to one's work, one's self and one's passion.

Myth 5: Inviting passionate educational leadership is just stuff professors write about in books like this. There are countless numbers of real live educators who put this theory of practice to work in their schools every day. Perhaps to get a better sense of inviting passionate leadership one should see such leaders in action. One could go to Hong Kong and see Principal Clio Chan and her magically inviting staff at Creative Primary School. One could go to Calcium, New York, and see Principal Lana Taylor and the innovative staff of Calcium Primary School. One could go to Grand Island, Nebraska, and see Principal Kent Mann and the dedicated teachers and staff of Grand Island Secondary School. One could go to Scott County, Kentucky, and see Superintendent Dallas Blankenship and the amazing exchange programme developed with teachers from Hong Kong. Each of these practising leaders has received the Inviting School Award given by the Alliance for Invitational Education. One could go to more than one hundred other schools across the globe that have also received the award and see the imaginative acts of hope they have helped create (Novak, Rocca, and DiBiase, 2006).

Inviting passionate educational leadership does not demand perfection, but it does require the effort to appreciate the good that is being done and the desire to get better; it does not mean having to be 'on', but it does mean choosing to care about others and oneself and finding ways to harmonize the two; it does not mean being simplistic and thinking that good things have to happen, but it does mean getting to the essence of things and taking a positive and realistic approach; it does not mean being one particular prescribed way, but it does mean developing one's unique style and strengths; it does not mean that it can only be written about by professors of education, but it does mean finding creative ways to connect with others to make good things happen.

Inviting passionate educational leadership is an ideal, a theory and a method. It is a part of a larger project to realize more of human's potential and to call forth more imaginative and sustainable ways to live educational lives. It is practised by real people throughout the world and sustained by the International Alliance for Invitational Education. It is for those who desire to be strong of heart, deep of thought and determined of action. It is for those who seek deeper connections with people, ideas and adventures. It is for those who understand that you cannot really lead without passion, while also appreciating that you cannot really educate without understanding passion.

References

Anderson, W. (1990) *Reality isn't what it used to be: Theatrical Politics, Ready-to-Wear Religion, Global Myths, Primitive Chic, and Other Wonders of the Postmodern World.* San Francisco, CA: HarperCollins.

Camus, A. (1956) *The Rebel: An Essay on Man in Revolt.* New York: Alfred A. Knopf.

Combs, A. (1982) *A Personal Approach to Teaching: Beliefs that Make a Difference.* New York: Allyn & Bacon.

Crawford. C. (2007) *The Politics of Life: 25 Rules for Survival in a Brutal and Manipulative World.* Lanham, MD: Rowman & Littlefield.

Csikszentmihalyi, M. (1997) *Finding Flow: The Psychology of Engagement with Everyday Life.* New York: HarperCollins.

Dewey, J. (1929) *The Quest for Certainty.* New York: Minton, Balch.

Dewey, J. (1934) *Art as Experience*. New York: Minton, Balch.

Dewey, J. (1938) *Experience and Education*. New York: Macmillan.

Gardner, H. (1999) *The Disciplined Mind: What All Students Should Understand*. New York: Simon and Schuster.

Homer-Dixon, T. (2000) *The Ingenuity Gap*. New York: Alfred A. Knopf.

Kelly, G. (1963) *A Theory of Personality: The Psychology of Personal Constructs*. New York: W.W. Norton.

Merriam-Webster's Collegiate Dictionary 10th edn. (1993) Markham, ON: Thomas Allen & Son.

Mutz, D. (2006) *Hearing the Other Side: Deliberative Versus Participatory Democracy*. New York: Cambridge University Press.

Novak, J. (2002) *Inviting Educational Leadership: Fulfilling Potential and Applying an Ethical Perspective to the Educational Process*. London: Pearson.

Novak, J., Rocca, W., and DiBiase, A. (eds) (2006) *Creating Inviting Schools*. San Francisco, CA: Caddo Gap.

Perkins, D. (1992) *Smart Schools*. New York: Free Press.

Petrini, C. (2003) *Slow Food: The Case for Taste*. New York: Columbia University Press.

Purkey, W. (2000) *What Students Say to Themselves: Internal Dialogue and School Success*. Thousand Oaks, CA: Corwin Press.

Purkey, W. and Novak, J. (1996) *Inviting School Success: A Self-Concept Approach to Teaching, Learning, and Democratic Practice,* 3rd edn. Belmount, CA: Wadsworth.

Rorty, R. (1989) *Contingency, Irony, and Solidarity*. New York: Cambridge University Press.

Seligman, M. (2002) *Authentic Happiness: Using the New Positive Psychology to Realize Your Potential for Lasting Fulfillment*. New York: Free Press.

Shade, P. (2001) *Habits of Hope: A Pragmatic Theory*. Nashville, TN: Vanderbilt University Press.

Singer, P. (2002) *One World: The Ethics of Globalization*. New Haven, CN: Yale University Press.

Ury, W. (2007) *The Power of Positive No: How to Say No and Still Get to Yes*. New York: Bantam.

Chapter 3

'Reservoirs of hope': sustaining passion in leadership

Alan Flintham

In the 1986 film 'Clockwise', the manic headteacher, played by John Cleese, utters the memorable words: 'It's not the despair. I can take the despair. It's the *hope* I can't stand!' For when critical incidents hit schools, colleagues look to their leaders to continue to be the beacon of hope, to preserve the flame of positive vision when circumstances conspire to extinguish it. But to do this requires inner reserves in the school leader, which have to be replenished and sustained if their motivation and passion for leadership is to be preserved in such circumstances. So leaders have to have sustainability strategies to maintain their own inner self-belief and emotional reserves, to sustain them in the testing times when staying passionate in leadership becomes problematic.

Drawing on research, originally involving interviews with 40 headteachers under the auspices of the National College for School Leadership (NCSL) research associate scheme (Flintham, 2003a,b), but now extended to encompass discussions with 140 serving school leaders in both England and Australia, it has been possible to test and develop this concept by using the metaphor of 'reservoirs of hope' to describe school leadership. Such interviews have provided a non-judgemental opportunity for leaders to reflect on critical incidents in their leadership stories and to articulate what has sustained their passion for leadership in the face of such challenging pressures. They have validated the usefulness of the metaphor in promoting such reflection and drawing conclusions from it in terms of what underpins and sustains a passion for leadership even when that leadership is put to the test by external pressures. They have also hopefully enabled the capture, as shown in subsequent quotations from serving school leaders, of an authentic rendering of practitioner voice.

It is argued that the successful leader acts as the *external reservoir of hope* for the institution, because 'hope' is what drives the school forward towards delivering its vision in the face of external pressures whilst allowing it to remain true to its fundamental values. The school community looks to the headteacher to take actions which maintain the coherence of collective vision and integrity of values, and to preserve its sense of hope when faced with challenging circumstances which threaten to blow the school off-course. Such actions have to be imbued with vision yet anchored in reality, for in the words of a Japanese proverb: 'Vision without action is a daydream, but action without vision is a nightmare'. To be able to act in this way demands that the leader has an *internal reservoir of hope* (the phrase is from West-Burnham, 2002: 4, and is used by kind permission), the calm centre at the heart of the individual leader, 'the still point of the turning world' from which their values and vision flows and which continues to allow effective interpersonal engagement and sustainability of personal and institutional self-belief in the face of draining external pressures and challenging critical incidents in the life of the school.

It should however be noted that 'hope' in school leadership is not the same as 'optimism'. Optimism as 'a confident expectation that it will always come out right in the end' is easy in positive leadership situations; hope characteristically is what is required in the darkness of community tragedies, acute personnel problems and organizational crises when leadership is put to the test and there is no guarantee of a successful outcome. Hope is circumscribed by moral values in a way which optimism is not. Hope is constrained by an assessment of what is really important in a situation, not what appears to be important. Hope carries with it a commitment to action, which can in itself be further draining of emotion and energy from the internal reservoir (Watts, 2002: 138–9).

This personal reservoir of hope has therefore to be periodically refilled by a variety of replenishment and sustainability strategies, without which the result will be burn out or drop out and leaders will withdraw from the change arena, and in the memorable words of one headteacher, 'die a lingering death through managing the stock cupboard'.

This chapter therefore considers firstly the underpinning value systems identified by school leaders as providing the foundations of their internal reservoirs of hope. It moves on to describe the testing times when maintaining hope and a passion for leadership becomes more problematical as challenging circumstances and critical incidents threaten to drain the reservoir. It concludes by identifying the sustainability strategies used by school leaders to refill their personal reservoir of hope and how these are developed over time and as a function of experience to ensure that the passion for leadership remains undimmed.

The foundations of the reservoir of hope

The 'foundations of the reservoir', the spiritual, moral and ethical bases on which individual leadership stands and which provide the well-spring which motivates, replenishes and renews the passion for leadership, are provided by a clearly articulated value system which explicitly or implicitly underpins leadership actions. In 140 interviews conducted with school leaders in both England and Australia, none has been unable to articulate, instantly and often passionately, the value system which inspires and motivates their leadership.

Although deriving from a variety of faith perspectives and belief frameworks, that value system may be categorized as either generational, faith-based, or egalitarian, or a combination of these.

The *generational imperative* of leadership stems from a value system laid down by early upbringing. As Parker (2002: 3) has put it: 'How we work and how we lead depends to a significant extent on who we are, which in turn is a product of what we have been'. Many headteachers interviewed were first generation entrants to higher education. Many have indicated that their foundational values were laid down in often working class upbringings, 'which laid down core values of inclusivity'. That value system, coupled with a vision of education as 'a passport out of deprivation', had led to a consequent 'passion to make a difference' to the life chances of future generations. As one headteacher put it:

I'm here because someone made a difference for me, and that has led to a sense of duty to give something back, to make a difference like it made a difference for me.

This influence of family upbringing on present leadership actions was highlighted succinctly and movingly by a headteacher working in an area of significant social deprivation:

I'm here as away of saying 'thank you' to my dad for what he did for me ... and my actions are determined by the acid test of 'what would my dad think of this?'.

Faith-based value systems were cited by a number of headteachers as influencing their professional practice, creating a *faith-based imperative* for leadership actions. It is significant that this was not restricted to those serving in schools of a specific religious character, nor to participants engaged in active religious practice. For some, the guiding overtly religious value system was underpinned and supported by membership of a faith community, 'which feeds me through its worship and empowers me in service' and results in a perceived 'call to live out the message of the gospel to love one another'. For others, whilst the original motivational connection between the religious beliefs laid down in childhood and the present adult ethical value system had long since been broken, the erstwhile bedrock of values still remains, albeit divorced from any belief in the concept of a higher being, in what has been termed 'a godless morality' (Holloway 1999: 4). For all, however, there remained the responsibility of ensuring that leadership actions could be validly judged against the articulated value system: the need to ensure that 'the talk is walked'. As one headteacher put it:

Every leadership decision has to stand the test of comparison against your publicly avowed principles.

For many, irrespective of faith perspective, there was an *egalitarian imperative* which underpinned their leadership: a commitment to social justice, a belief in social inclusion and equality of opportunity and a sense that 'everyone has the potential to lead a good life ... the school's job is to realise that potential', a motivation pithily summed up in one school's mission statement: 'Everybody here can be somebody'.

That passionate egalitarian approach, inspired by a 'transference imperative' that tested professional leadership decisions against the personal yardstick of 'would I be happy if this were being done to my own children and if not, why I am I doing it to someone else's children?', is however often tinged with a realistic recognition of its potential costs. This was articulated by one headteacher as follows:

I want to make a difference, although I know it will mean going the extra mile. You've got to have the courage to take risks, to risk that it may all go wrong, and not to compromise just to meet the expectations of others or the system. If you feel OK inside about it, that it is true to your values, then you know you are right.

The 'passion to make a difference', no matter what the professional cost, is particularly but not exclusively exemplified by those leading schools facing challenging circumstances (Flintham, 2006). Headteachers of such schools are energized by challenge and a capacity to make a difference both to their schools and also the communities in which they are set. They have a passionate belief in the potential for success of their schools, even if that might be 'success against the odds'. Particularly in schools facing challenging circumstances, it is felt that an impact can be made straightaway, with the opportunity to make rapid changes and see significant and fast improvement, making the ratio of effort to progress seem more advantageous: 'there is so far to go that it is easier to move forward'. And that movement forward provides in itself both motivation and catalyst for further development: 'you can have small tastes of success ... and they taste good, so you want more'.

Headteachers not only relish the capacity to have such immediate impact and secure rapid and tangible progress within a receptive change environment, they are energized by the excitement and unpredictability of the role:

Schools are exciting places to be: you are the driving force with the power to make a difference and add value to the life chances of children and the community, and to empower others to do the same.

This becomes highly addictive:

You get hooked on the buzz from seeing people achieve, develop and grow, and that is enhanced by 'the strangely alluring adrenaline rush of not knowing what is going to happen next!'

Headteachers are driven by core values which are people-centred and founded on effective relationships. They combine moral purpose with a high respect for others and a strong belief in the capacity of all to succeed within an inclusive environment. They accept there are times when these core values are buffeted by the pressures of external events and it is necessary to remain firm. In schools facing challenging pupil behaviour and pressures militating against inclusion, it is, 'sometimes necessary to remind your staff that these are your lines in the sand ... to state that these are my values; you need to stand with me on this', even though there might be an operational price to be paid in staff recruitment or retention as a result of the moral stand being taken.

In essence, it is felt necessary to 'stick with your convictions, to make clear what you believe in and stick with it ... or you will not survive'. Often the experience of having to do so was a personally developing one for headteachers. As one headteacher testified:

The experience [of facing a critical incident] shook my belief system about what I stand for, but then paradoxically led to a reaffirmation and strengthening of what my core values actually are.

Draining the reservoir

Serving headteachers face an extensive range, frequency and depth of day-to-day pressures and unexpected and challenging critical incidents. Such pressures call upon them to display sustained high-level leadership qualities and maintain their passion for the role, yet threaten to drain their personal reservoir of hope. Headteachers are able to offer compelling micro-narratives of situations they have been called upon to face where they felt such draining pressures, and have valued the opportunity to reflect on what had sustained them through the situation.

The opportunity to recount such experiences in a non-judge-mental and supportive forum has proved to be a cathartic and liberating experience, and equally the opportunity to hear such leadership stories from colleagues in similar circumstances has provided a powerful support mechanism in itself to combat the isolation of leadership and maintain the passion for it. As one headteacher put it:

> *Wrapping it up in a story makes it more powerful and memorable. It gives you self confidence and an awareness that you are not alone in having had to face such circumstances.*

Whilst it would be inappropriate to engage in precise contextual detail, critical incidents described by headteachers can be classified as encompassing community tragedies, personnel problems and organizational crises.

As regards *community tragedies*, schools and their leaders are long used to dealing with anticipated death through the loss of pupils, staff and parents from long-term illness, and having to keep the school on emotional track through the process of loss, bereavement and beyond. More difficult to deal with are the unexpected deaths, often sudden, violent or self-inflicted. Schools and their leaders in such circumstances find themselves in the eye of the storm, with the school being seen as, 'the community space in which to grieve and reflect in mutual sympathy and support'.

An inner confidence in one's ability to cope with the situation, a personal reservoir of hope that progress through it can be maintained, and an empathetic concern for the strength of relationships with all who are caught up in it, whilst articulated in different ways, provide the essential characteristics which enable school leaders to deal with the aftermath of such tragedies. They are required to call upon high levels of personal emotional resilience and leadership skills in order to deal with the community implications of such loss, not simply within the school itself but also within the wider community that the school serves. Headteachers dealing with such events find themselves in the front line of maintaining community relationships often fractured by anger and grief. In responding to such circumstances, the school provides 'an oasis of calm in a troubled community', an oasis which is clearly watered by the well-spring of values of the leaders themselves as they act not only as external reservoirs of hope for their schools, but also for the communities in which they are set.

Equally draining if somewhat less critical are the *personnel problems* which are part of the day-to-day lot of the school leader, be they child protection issues, allegations of assault or staff redundancies, wherein much work needs to be done unobtrusively at a personal level to maintain morale when the full details of the situation, or what is being done behind the scenes to resolve it, cannot be made public, and ill-informed criticism of leadership actions becomes endemic. In such circumstances, the headteacher's primary aim must be 'restoring the community and leading it on', whilst recognizing the draining effect on their own personal internal reservoir and the consequent need not only to maintain an inner equilibrium and faith in the rightness of one's actions when measured against the greater good, but also to supplement that inner self-belief by consciously engaging in compensatory post-hoc replenishment strategies.

Organizational crises to do with the running of the school, and operational decisions taken in matters such as dress code, pupil exclusion or external inspection, with all the ensuing potential publicity implications which can result, also test the reservoir of hope of leaders, with the dual need both to retain continuing internal self-confidence and integrity and to ensure the retention of agreed institutional values in the face of such pressures. There is the necessity to remain the perceived centre of calm for the school community, even at some innerpersonal cost in unseen emotional turbulence: what could be described as the 'swan syndrome', apparently calm and serene on the surface whilst paddling like mad underneath!

One headteacher described the personal hidden emotional cost of such behaviour:

> *I didn't let go until a week later [after a difficult OFSTED inspection], after I was sure that everyone else was alright. Then I went home that weekend and cracked up. It took me the weekend to re-establish my values base, but by Monday morning I was OK.*

This gives a further example of the capacity of the successful school leader to continue to act as the external reservoir of hope as the first priority, and then to return thereafter to rebuild and refill the internal sustaining reservoir that makes the continuance of such behaviour possible.

With hindsight, however, many school leaders found that such testing through critical incidents was in itself a learning and developmental experience in terms of growth in emotional resilience and leadership confidence. This engendered a feeling that, 'if I can deal with that, I can deal with anything' and a concomitant sense that the school becomes collectively stronger too. It was felt that:

> *Nothing succeeds like success against the odds in building inner confidence and in building hope in the school.*

Most headteachers, however, were thankful that such unsought learning experiences had not come earlier in their leadership careers, recognizing the growth in confidence, self-awareness and willingness to use more creative and adventurous solutions whilst remaining true to their value system that they could now display. Many identified with a perceived 'sea change' in headship as their experience had deepened, with a move from 'doing headship' into 'being the head'. This experience base not only gave more confidence in dealing with the mechanics of headship, it also allowed a shift in focus towards being more concerned with reflecting upon and articulating the values governing leadership actions and the development of the relationships which facilitated their effective implementation.

As one experienced headteacher summed it up: 'I now know how to *be* a head as opposed to doing the headship job. It's the difference between knowing the words and knowing the tune'. This in turn impacted upon how she related to her staff, with a sense of, 'now being able to "feel" the tune when you are dealing with people', even when the pressures of unexpected events threaten to turn leadership into 'more of a rap than an aria!'.

Refilling the reservoir

The personal reservoir of hope of headteachers has to be periodically refilled against the draining effect of external pressures, by a variety of replenishing and sustaining strategies, without which the implementation of the espoused value system will fail, the intensity of passion in leadership fade, and withdrawal from the task of leading change occur.

Headteachers utilize a range of personal and corporate sustaining strategies to guard against this. These may be categorized as:

- belief networks
- support networks
- external networks.

Belief networks

Belief networks of like-minded colleagues imbued with similar value systems who can provide affirmative feedback are felt to be essential and their support is to be captured at all costs: 'You jockey for position as to who to sit next to at heads' conferences. You need to be alongside someone on the same wavelength as you are'.

Such affirmative support comes not only from colleagues but from parents, governors and from what is felt to be the core of the job, the pupils: 'children are a touchstone; I walk round [the school] and draw strength from their reactions', said one inner-city headteacher, and Woods (2002: 14) in his seminal study of 'enchanted heads' who remain committed and enthusiastic after many years of service, reports on 'a passionate outpouring of anecdotes' from his primary colleagues as to the joy of being with children and seeing them thrive, especially in demanding social circumstances.

Support networks

Support networks of families, particularly long-suffering partners, and friends also sustain the inner reservoir of hope. Some colleagues are able to 'compartmentalize' the problems of the day so that they do not leak across into home life; others value the existence of 'a sounding board' at home as a catharsis to verbalize and off-load the events of the day; others are adamant that they would not do this but know nevertheless that the support is there.

One headteacher was prepared to go as far as to state that: 'I don't see how you can go home on your own at night and come back the next day sane'. Others, however, paid testimony to the value of, 'talking it through with the dog (who always seems to agree) on early morning walks' or valued the opportunities of 'conversations with yourself' on the long drive home.

Many headteachers recognize the need to create the capacity for strategic reflection opportunities where it is possible to re-examine and renew a personal value system through the challenge and support of a fellow practitioner, who can act as 'a detached sounding board, with similar experience, who is a good listener but who can also plant the key questions to aid formative reflection'. They thus valued the opportunity for a peer support relationship with a colleague headteacher acting as 'a professional listening and learning partner'. This was deemed to be more valuable than mentoring or coaching, with its implications of a more senior, experienced colleague supporting a more junior one, and was felt to be a more symbiotic and mutually beneficial relationship, providing the cathartic spiritual support of a 'soul friend'.

It was felt that it should not be necessary for a school leader to have to be pro-active in seeking out such peer support, and potentially feeling guilty for accessing it. Rather it should be provided as part of an entitlement within a leadership support package for those who wish to avail themselves of it. An example of this philosophy translated into action is to be found in operation within Nottinghamshire Local Authority in England, where a peer support scheme known as 'Heads Count' offers to serving school leaders of whatever length of experience the opportunity of participating in a paired professional relationship with a colleague headteacher trained in listening and emotional intelligence skills, in a mutually beneficial scheme free at the point of delivery (Flintham, 2007). There is also some parallel with the 'Principals First' scheme operating in Melbourne, Australia, which provides both professional mentoring and counselling support on health and well-being issues from a team of recently retired principals, albeit on a costed subscription basis.

Such personal support was not seen to be drawn only from other headteachers, nor indeed just senior leadership colleagues within the school. Several headteachers would also identify with the benefit of 'the day-to-day support of the office staff in providing tea, sympathy and laughter' as a welcome antidote to the pressures of the day.

Similarly, the opportunity to engage in corporate networks of colleagues is valued, especially if they are of a similar mindset: 'a supportive network of like-minded colleagues from schools in similar circumstances and facing similar issues, and where you can have an open honest relationship based more on support than challenge'. Such networks, often self-generated rather than externally imposed, develop 'an ad hoc networked learning community' which provides not only cathartic personal nurturing support, mutual reflection opportunities and information flow, but also a bulwark against a perceived sense of isolation in headship, particularly when working in pressurized or challenging circumstances.

External networks

External networks of engagement with interests and experiences beyond education provide what could be called the 'hinterland of headship', following Denis Healey who was accused of having 'too much hinterland for a politician' (Healey, 1990: 564). It is, however, ironic that in order to create a reservoir in the first place, vast tracts of hinterland have to be submerged, external interests lost, relationships strained and friendships forsaken, in order to create the single-mindedness of vision thought necessary to aspire to and succeed in headship. Then, somewhat paradoxically, it is such interests and relationships that have to be reacquired or regenerated in order to provide the sustaining strategies needed for continuing survival of its pressures.

Experienced headteachers therefore strive to preserve at all costs their hinterland, valuing a capacity to 'get away from it all by disappearing into something else'. That 'something else' often involves participation in relaxation and renewal opportunities far removed from the professional role. Some valued 'the precious 38 minutes [the effective capacity of an oxygen tank] out of communication whilst scuba diving' or the 'masochistic satisfaction' of supporting the local football team. Others, in spite of working a self-confessed '60–70 hour week', found satisfaction in the opportunity of participating in the local soup run to the disadvantaged and homeless, and appreciated the chance to refocus on 'a world elsewhere', far removed from the particular pressures of the school situation.

Such participation reinforced a firm belief in the importance of 'compartmentalization' as a sustaining strategy in preserving both personal integrity and the passion for leadership. As one Australian school principal trenchantly put it:

> *You cannot be a successful school leader if you are only involved in school life. Don't live to work … work to live!*

Confronting the 'plateau effect'

Whilst for some school leaders it is the unexpected additional pressure of facing an unanticipated critical incident situation which makes compartmentalization of emotions difficult and threatens to overwhelm the defences of the reservoir, for others it is the long-term relentless repeated pressure of the continual waves of change, and an accompanying sense of *déjà vu* in having to revisit circumstances already previously experienced, that wears down the reservoir's retaining wall. If there is an acceptance of the sea change in leadership around the 4–5 year mark with the transition from 'doing' to 'being', then equally there is a recognition amongst experienced headteachers of the emergence of a 'plateau effect' around 7–10 years in post, with a potential decline in effectiveness as leadership becomes 'a chore not a challenge' (Earley, 2006: 15).

To confront the plateau effect and to preserve the passion against the jaundice of excessive experience requires re-energizing professional refreshment and renewal activities to be provided or sought out. One colleague argued for the need to, 'develop an area of interest and expertise outside your school and fertilise it. It benefits you and it benefits the school'. There was an appreciation of the benefit to other senior leaders too, with one experienced headteacher advising: 'Seek professional time away from headship. You renew your reservoir away from the school and there is a development of the others who are left behind managing the school in your absence'. There was, however, a sage recognition of the need to preserve a balance between personal fulfilment and the organizational needs of the school, and the danger of what could be termed 'the absentee landlord syndrome'.

For some, however, confronting the plateau effect is best done by ensuring that it never arrives in the first place. An emerging post-modernist generation of school leaders can be identified with a world view which does not necessarily envisage linear career pro-gression nor extended periods of headship service, but rather sees career development as a series of short-term professional portfolios constructed as appropriate to the multitude of settings encountered.

In common with the post-modernist generation of computer-confident students in our schools, who recognize the exponentially advancing nature of the technology with which they engage and have the confidence and flexibility constantly to be prepared to update their skills set in order to be able to surf the constant waves of change that it brings, such emergent 'post-modernist portfolio principals' (Flintham, 2004) do not see school leadership as neces-sarily a job for life, but as a series of emerging opportunities requiring different clusters of professional skills and strengths within a limited time frame.

Consequently, they have a pro-active exit strategy planned to move on into other facets of educational life before the plateau effect kicks in. Such headteachers are characterized by having robust short-term sustainability strategies coupled with the ability to com-partmentalize their feelings, be pro-active in their responses to external pressures, and the capacity to disengage from school lead-ership once they feel their task is complete and 'before the fruit begins to rot on the vine'.

The privilege and the price of principalship

A study of school principals' workload and its impact on health and well-being, conducted for the Australian Department of Education and Training of the State of Victoria (Saulwick and Muller, 2004), was aptly named *The Privilege and the Price*. It found that principals almost universally 'love their job' and think of themselves as having the 'privilege' of caring for and developing young people and their fami-lies. A number of respondents in the survey indicated that a commitment to the people in their care will usually take precedence over everything else, be it demands from outside the caring relationship, monetary reward or personal preferment. The 'price', however, is an inherent leadership tension between this caring imperative and the managerial demands of the role: what the report calls 'the carer versus manager tension' (Saulwick and Muller, 2004: 22).

A study conducted by the Australian Catholic University (ACU National), (Duignan et al., 2005) into socially responsible indicators for policy, practice and benchmarking for human service organizations, also identified similar potential tensions between economic and social imperatives. The study contrasts a managerial economic efficiency orientation, driven by a concern for competences, targets and measurable outcomes, with a caring, socially responsible imperative, with indicators of service, care, stewardship and trust.

The chief investigator in this study, writing in another context, argues that authentic leaders earn the respect of their colleagues not through performance compliance: 'Leaders *earn* their allegiance through authentic actions and interactions in trusting relationships' (Duignan, 2003: 2).

In no circumstances is that trust called upon more fully than when critical incidents hit a school community. In terms of the metaphor of 'reservoirs of hope' as applied to school leadership, the *'privilege of principalship'* in such circumstances is to be trusted as the external reservoir of hope for the school. The *'price of principalship'* is the potential draining of the personal internal reservoir of hope by being called upon so to do.

Investing in the support and sustainability of principals regarding the leadership they are called upon to exercise in such circumstances is a sound investment when compared to the potential human cost of burn-out or under functioning. And such investment would not only reinforce the *privilege* of principalship and enhance the ease of recruitment to it, and redeem the *price* of it paid in terms of human commitment, but it would also retain amongst its adherents the *passion* for leadership which drew them into the role in the first place and which is needed to sustain their continuance in it.

References

Duignan, P.A. (2003) 'Authenticity in Leadership: Encouraging the Heart, Celebrating the Spirit', paper presented to the Lutheran Principals National Conference, Canberra.

Duignan, P.A, Butcher, J., Spies-Butcher, B. and Collins, J.F. (2005) *Socially Responsible Indicators for policy, practice and benchmarking in service organisations.* Sydney: ACU National.

Earley, P. (2006) *Headship and Beyond: The motivation and development of school leaders.* Professorial Lecture delivered at the Institute of Education, University of London.

Flintham, A.J. (2003a) *Reservoirs of Hope: Spiritual and moral leadership in headteachers.* National College for School Leadership Practitioner Enquiry Report. Nottingham: NCSL.

Flintham, A.J. (2003b) *When Reservoirs Run Dry: Why some headteachers leave headship early.* National College for School Leadership Practitioner Enquiry Report. Nottingham: NCSL.

Flintham, A.J. (2004) 'Post-Modernist Portfolio People: Sustainability and succession in school leadership', *Management in Education* 11(3): 16–19.

Flintham, A.J. (2006) *What's Good About Leading Schools in Challenging Circumstances?* Nottingham: NCSL.

Flintham, A.J. (2007) 'Nottinghamshire Head Teacher Peer Support: A model for headteacher collaboration, sustainability, and development', in *Head Teachers of the Future*, Bagshot, *Westminster Education Forum*, pp. 46–8.

Healey, D. (1990) *The Time of My Life.* London: Penguin.

Holloway, R. (1999) *Godless Morality: Keeping Religion out of Ethics.* Edinburgh: Canongate.

Parker, R. (2002) *Passion and Intuition: The impact of life history on leadership.* National College for School Leadership Practitioner Enquiry Report. Nottingham: NCSL.

Saulwick, I. and Muller, D. (2004) *The Privilege and the Price: A study of Principal Class Workload and its Impact on Health and Well Being; Final Report.* State Government of Victoria, Department of Education and Training.

Watts, F.N. (2002) *Theology and Psychology.* Aldershot: Ashgate.

West-Burnham, J. (2002) *Leadership and Spirituality.* National College for School Leadership Leading Edge Seminar Thinkpiece. Nottingham: NCSL.

Woods, R. (2002) *Enchanted Headteachers: Sustainability in Primary School Headship.* National College for School Leadership Practitioner Enquiry Report. Nottingham: NCSL.

Section three

Research on passionate leadership

Chapter 4

Successful leadership: An intelligent passion

Christopher Day[1]

Until recently, much of the writing about leadership seems to be oriented either towards the passion of purpose and person, embracing what might be called generically 'emotional' leadership; or it focuses upon the cognitive, behavioural, observable aspects. More recently, and perhaps not surprisingly in the context of countries in which radical policy intervention by governments has led to high stakes, testable, results-driven student attainment cultures in schools, the traditional territory of leadership research seems to have become occupied by school effectiveness research, which has tended to focus upon what conditions exist that either hinder or help promote student outcomes, usually expressed as their attainments, which can be measured by tests and examinations. They essentially – albeit independently – service the many headed 'Hydra' of nationally driven school improvement by providing evaluation research which seeks to identify whether or not there are any cause and effect or associative relationships between the measurement of results of schools for pupils at different stages and its contexts, inputs and processes. This latter movement is often criticized as being insufficiently attentive to critical social discourses of the nature and context of schooling and thus essentially uncritically justifying, if not supporting, government initiatives. The growing plethora of research, each with its own traditions and adherents, seems to cloud rather than clarify the nature of successful school leadership, providing assertive, authoritative, but usually partial advice. In recent years in England, the establishment of a National College of School

Leadership (NCSL) has begun to draw these 'behavioural', 'affective' and 'effectiveness' strands together in developing its training and development programmes, but has not yet quite 'bottled' the secrets of success.

My own readings and involvement over many years now in research on successful school leadership lead me to believe that it needs both intelligence and passion, and that successful leaders themselves hold values which encompass an abiding belief in social equity – that all children and young people are entitled to the best teaching from the best teachers in the best learning environments; that all learners are able to achieve (in the broadest sense) and attain (by means of whatever tests and examinations are currently available); and that it is their job to ensure that this happens. They know that in order for this to happen they have to exercise 'intelligent passion' – though they may not call it that. This chapter is a story of such passion in action.

> *Good teachers (leaders) possess a capacity for connectedness. They are able to weave a complex web of connections among themselves, their subjects and their students (teachers) so that students (teachers) can learn to weave a world for themselves.* (Palmer, 1995: 11)

An ongoing 12-country, international research project which focuses upon successful headteachers, has found that they display, through who they are and how they act, a deep and passionate commitment to their work (Day and Leithwood, 2007). No matter what the circumstances or challenges which they faced, they had sustained their passion for education, and within this, their passionate desire for the success of all their students. This was communicated directly through their sense of humour, interpersonal warmth, patience, empathy and support of their staff, parents' and pupils' self-esteem and a capacity for continued reflection of different kinds.

Passion

Passion is defined in the *Oxford English Dictionary* (1989) as 'any kind of feeling by which the mind is powerfully affected or moved'.

It is a driver, a motivational force emanating from strength of emotion. People are passionate about things, issues, causes, and people. Being passionate generates energy, determination, conviction, commitment and even obsession in people. Passion is not a luxury, a frill, or a quality possessed by just a few headteachers. It is essential to all successful leadership. Often what drives passionate feelings is unconscious: Behind the ordered control and professional calm of headteachers, bubble:

> ... *deep, potentially explosive passions, emotions bringing despair, elation, anger and joy of a kind not normally associated in the public mind with work.* (Nias, 1996: 226)

Such passion was evident in the study of ten successful headteachers working in schools in disadvantaged communities in England (Day, 2005). Their passion was expressed both through their enthusiasm, and also through principled, values-led, leadership. Like effective teachers, these headteachers had a passion for their schools, a passion for their pupils and a passionate belief that who they were and how they led could make a difference in the lives of staff, pupils, parents and the community, both in the moments of leadership and in the days, weeks, months and even years afterwards. Passion was associated with enthusiasm for achievement, caring, collaboration, commitment, trust, inclusivity and courage which are themselves key characteristics of effectiveness in teaching.

Passion was also associated with fairness and understanding, qualities constantly named by students in their assessments also of good teachers, and with the qualities that effective headteachers display in everyday social interactions – listening to what staff and students say, being close rather than distant, having a good sense of playfulness, humour, encouraging staff and students to learn in different ways, relating learning to experience, encouraging all to take a collegial responsibility for learning, maintaining organized school and classroom environments, being knowledgeable about their work, creating learning environments which engaged both staff and students and stimulated in them an excitement to learn.

Six areas of passion were identified through the data gathered from those interviewed in the study:

1. A passion for achievement
2. A passion for care
3. A passion for collaboration
4. A passion for commitment
5. A passion for trust
6. A passion for inclusivity.

A passion for achievement

> *I get this feeling of passion, almost like a passion for the school. I sense a feeling that she feels something that when the school achieves that she has achieved in order for the school to be achieving ... she has always had a strong desire to maintain or improve standards and to better the school ... to see that people are able to achieve.* (Parent)

This comment by a parent about the headteacher of a 1,200 strong comprehensive school near London where almost half the pupils receive free school meals, is typical of the high personal and professional investment made in their schools by ten English headteachers in schools in challenging economic and social environments, who with their colleagues, pupils, parents and governors, participated in an eight-country project on successful school leadership. The catchment area for the school was classified as among the most deprived 10 per cent in England with high unemployment. Students were described by the head as having, 'low attainment on entry, with some challenging behaviour'. The most recent Ofsted report had described the school as 'very good, with a number of outstanding areas, including a behaviour management policy'. The school also had a good student attendance rate and high teacher retention – both key factors in successful schools.

Helen had been headteacher for 13 years. How, then, did this headteacher's passion express itself? What were the key indicators of success that might be attributed to this elusive quality? First, it is necessary to define what passion is and why it is essential to successful leadership.

> *The example we set as passionate adults allows us to connect to [pupils'] minds and spirits in a way that we can have a lasting, pos-*

itive impact on their lives ... by ... working with the [pupils] at the frontier of their own individual and collective experiences, feelings and opinions. (Fried, 1995: 27–8)

It is this passion which is rarely acknowledged as being at the heart of the intellectual endeavours and emotional commitment to service of teachers and headteachers as they work towards the moral purposes of society through students and young people. For Helen, success with the school, which has a 93 per cent ethnic minority population (with 58 languages spoken, and 87 per cent speaking a language other than English at home) was multi-faceted. Achievement took time. One part of it was defined as:

... getting in the top 5 per cent (of A–Cs at GCSE level). It was the culmination of everything that we'd hoped for and worked for ... we had to work really hard to get the 'technology' status ... the staff didn't believe we could do it, but it worked for us. (Headteacher)

However, Helen, like other successful headteachers in the study, had 'lifted' the school in a number of different ways. When she had arrived, the school was the least popular in the area, the examination results 'terrible'. These had improved from 12 per cent A–Cs to 65 per cent over the period. Students staying on at the school beyond the statutory school leaving age had increased from 84 to 300. Her values were clear:

... the one thing which struck me when I came here first was that the children were getting a raw deal ... there wasn't any focus on achievement at all ...

Helen described herself as having, a great personal interest in children, and her particular style of leadership as being 'child-centred'. She found the children very rewarding, 'even the rogues and vagabonds'. She spoke of her interest in her pupils:

There's always something I involve myself in to do with children. I always eat in the dining room ... I stand on the corridors ... I mostly take paperwork home ... I talk to people face-to-face.

This was confirmed by others in the school.

> *She likes motivating others and keeping them on the right track.* (Student)

> *You always see her wandering around. She's always around and about.* (Student)

> *She's achieved a lot for the school, and aims high.* (Student)

A passion for care

These actions were examples of a passion for caring which went far beyond duty. One of the teachers in the school provided an example of Helen's response to students' emotional needs and her belief that their education should not suffer:

> *An 11-year-old girl had a baby. The head arranged child care for the baby so the girl could do her GCSEs and ... she was quite clear that this girl's educational chances were not going to be ruined and the school was going to facilitate that girl at all costs and that's what happened.* (Teacher)

Successful headteachers in this study *liked* children and young people, felt comfortable talking with them, were interested in learning about their backgrounds and present realities, treated them as individuals and listened actively to what they said and how they acted. In short, a core part of their passion was care. Nel Noddings describes this as 'one-caring' in which:

> *Apprehending the other's reality, feeling what he feels as nearly as possible, is the essential part of caring ... For if I take on the other's reality as possibility and begin to feel its reality, I feel, also, that I must act accordingly; that is, I am impelled to act as though on my own behalf, but on behalf of the other.* (Noddings, 1984: 228)

Caring, as part of a passion for teaching is a key construct in the accounts given by pupils of all ages of good teachers. They are 'helpful', 'fair', 'encouraging', 'interested and enthusiastic', as against bad teachers who are 'indifferent' to the individual (Hargreaves D, 1972; Nash, 1973; Woods, 1979). Caring relationships are fundamental to successful leadership.

It is difficult to envisage a passionate leader without such professional integrity and whose first priority is not 'connectedness' with pupils, colleagues and self. Without this, motivation, trust and enthusiasm cannot be nurtured. In leadership in the school, as in leadership in the classroom, care and compassion are essential features of becoming and remaining connected to students and colleagues. Teachers and students alike work better when they are cared 'about': an expression of headteachers' personal beliefs and emotional commitment which goes beyond the contractual obligation of caring 'for' (Fletcher-Campbell, 1995).

A passion for collaboration

Much has been written about the relationship between effective teaching and school culture. It is now the 'received wisdom', for example, that collaborative cultures enhance teacher participation and that distributed leadership in this and across a wider range of stakeholders, including students, is likely to lead to and sustain teacher commitment. The headteachers in this study placed huge emotional investment – nurturing the capacities and capabilities of students, teachers, ancillaries, governors and parents as equal partners in the enterprise of teaching, learning and achievement. In other words, their aspirations were to build and sustain their schools as communities of teaching and learning, to make their schools good at learning (OECD, 2001a: 3). Such communities actively promote teamwork, networking, risk-taking, continuing professional development and participation through cultures of trust and collaboration which co-exist with decentralization, accountability, marketization and audit cultures encapsulated by the term 'new public management' (OECD, 2001b) and the current narrow usage of input–output 'effectiveness' success criteria.

This role has, arguably, become even more important as the social capital generated by families, neighbourhoods, communities and other networks tends to shrink in many countries. (OECD, 2001a: 47–8)

All those in the study focused upon teamwork as a means of draw-ing upon and building a fund of social capital, in order to create a store of shared experiences and foster individual and collective qualities and achievement, increase flexibility of response to change, and emphasize mutual responsiveness and collective responsibility. What is clear from the data, however, is that such teamworking was not encouraged as a means of sharing superficial-ity or self-protection. It was not regarded as a replacement for individual knowledge, experience and judgement but rather a com-plement to these. Teams in these schools had both power and authority in conjunction with the headteacher within an ethic of shared responsibility.

Little is known about the ways headteachers share power and authority with others without abandoning responsibility for progress. The data in this study reveal the structures of teamworking as com-plex and principled processes in the exercise of successful leadership.

> *We work really hard at supporting each other and watching each other learn, modelling lessons and saying, 'What did you think of this?' ... But you can't do it unless you've got a team of people who are willing to go along with you ... People who share the view that standards really do matter.* (Headteacher of primary school)

There was a sense of a collective rather than individual will to succeed:

> *It's got the system, it's got the monitoring, it's got data on kids, it's got systems in terms of 'pastoral care'; it's got monitoring in terms of standards, it's got lesson observation, [the school] got good practice, it's got INSET (In-Service Education and Training) for staff.* (Head-teacher of secondary school)

All headteachers focused much of their energy upon creating an ethos of mutual respect and developing the expectation within the schools that progress and standards were the responsibilities of all staff. The examples below are indicative of this focus:

> *This is not a one person act. I'm surrounded by able managers; 12 out of 14 heads of department are outstanding managers in their own right.* (Headteacher of secondary school)

I say to staff, 'You're all leaders because you lead your area of the curriculum. You are a manager too. You manage your classroom. (Headteacher of primary school)

A passion for commitment

It's involving as many people as want to be involved and my experience is that if you do involve them and if you do take things on board, you get even more back ... That's why it has to be teamwork with a capital 'T' from the very top to the bottom. (Headteacher of secondary school)

All the headteachers in the study had made 'room to manoeuvre' as external reform initiatives (which have the effect of reducing their range of discretionary judgements) were imposed and as the bureaucracy associated with increased contractual accountability began to bite. Such leaders survive and continue to flourish in the most challenging circumstances principally because of the strength of the values they hold and their willingness and ability to be creative, sometimes in the face of enormous constraints.

Part of the reason that successful heads in the study were able to continue to adapt and to move on in changing circumstances, was their awareness of, adherence to, and action on particular core values which focused upon 'making a positive difference' in the level of commitment of those with whom they worked.

Mr ... is the best thing that's happened to this school. [Before he came] we were in serious trouble and then we got a great report when the inspectors came round. He's so happy about it. Every time we're in assembly he always brings it up one way or another. He always says this is the best school he's ever been to. (Pupil of secondary school)

She has the ideas. She's the leader. She delegates. But you can't just say it's down to her 'cos it is down to every single member of staff, 'cos if she had a wonderful idea and the staff didn't fall for it and pull together it wouldn't be successful. We all agree with her vision and we all think, 'Yes, we can do it.' We've all got the ambition. (Teacher of primary school)

I suppose he's the anchor. The whole team of teachers works for him and he obviously holds it all together. He seems to have a lot of time for the staff and the parents and the children. I just think he's very passionate about what he does. He wants the school to do well. He wants the children to do well. I think that's what drives him. (Parent of primary school pupil)

For these headteachers, 'commitment' was made up of a combination of factors, the most important of which were:

1. A clear, enduring set of values and ideologies which inform practice regardless of social context.
2. The active rejection of a minimalist approach to leadership (to just doing the job).
3. A continuing willingness to reflect upon experience and the context in which practice occurs and to be adaptable.
4. A sustained sense of identity and purpose and an ability to find room to manoeuvre by managing tensions.
5. Intellectual and emotional engagement with all stakeholders.

A passion for trust

Especially evident in the comments during interviews with all stakeholders were the exercise of trust, focus upon teachers' motivation and self-efficacy and the emphasis on the creation and sustained building of productive, participative community relationships, all strong features of most recent conceptions of transformational leadership. Teacher after teacher referred to a school climate in which the headteacher 'trusts you implicitly and will let you deal with things ... you don't feel as if you've been infringed in any way'.

It's not just the pupils, it seems the staff are happy here too. He conveys strong leadership in everything. He's out there even after school, keeping an eye on things. He leads by example. He's got everybody's trust. He sort of relates that everything is under control and he's got his team well enthused. All the staff appear to be very happy and very committed. If it wasn't for his leadership, they wouldn't be. (Parent of secondary school pupil)

> *... the ease and friendliness is based upon the understanding that we behave professionally. We turn up on time, we mark our books, and we care about the school. If all that is taken as read, then we can have a good time with each other. And it means I don't give people a hard time if their results are down one year ...* (Headteacher of secondary school)

This kind of activist professionalism is premised on three concepts: trust, active trust and generative politics (Sachs, 2003: 138). Active trust is 'dependent on new kinds of social and professional relationships where different parts of the educational enterprise work together in strategic ways ... [It] requires that a shared set of values, principles and strategies is debated and negotiated' (Sachs, 2003: 140).

> *A fundamental feature of generative politics is that it allows and encourages individuals and groups to make things happen rather than to let things happen to them in the context of overall social concerns and goals.* (Sachs, 2003: 144)

Hargreaves (1994: 424) adds that active trust means that teachers 'feel a stronger obligation towards and responsibility for their colleagues'.

A passion for inclusivity

Headteachers positively encouraged all members of the school community to build a sense of community, continuity and purpose through creating sustained narratives of experience; and in doing so countered the temptations of seeking short-term solutions to long-term problems.

Each school, each headteacher, had their unique sense of communal identity – what Thomson in her work on *Schooling the Rustbelt Kids* (2002) has called the 'thisness' of schools – within the discontinuities of the environment. Each headteacher had constructed, with others, a coherent collage out of the multitude of policy reforms, fragmentation of work, changes in society, and seemingly, 'ceaseless rotation of elements' (Sennett, 1998: 134) present in and around their communities of practice which threaten to corrode them.

Under the leadership of these headteachers all the schools had increased the involvement of the parents in school and classroom matters, so that 'team' had become defined as encompassing the whole community:

> *There's a true community spirit here.* (Governor of secondary school)

> *There's a real community feeling. The vision is that the school is as successful as possible for the children and the community.* (Deputy headteacher of primary school)

In this primary school there were one-parent families, high unemployment and a lack of home support for pupils. Yet there was a strong community spirit fostered by the school.

> *We have parents coming in to do community courses – science, literacy and numeracy – so that they could help with the children.* (Teacher of primary school)

The headteacher had established a parents' room and employed a home–school liaison worker. One headteacher of a school in which 'the majority of children are under achieving before they come to school' (Teacher of primary school) referred to his style as 'Bill Shankly' management, after the manager of Liverpool's most successful football team:

> *If you keep telling people how good they are they start to believe it and once they start believing it then you can actually change things because you can give them the realization that they've got a lot to offer. They are the first educators of the children after all, and we only come in at a later date.* (Headteacher of primary school)

All made a heavy investment in regular contact with parents. In each school parents spoke of the genuine welcome, the time given to them unreservedly, and their appreciation of the facilities and opportunities to contribute to the pupils' and their own learning:

I can come to see the head or any of the other teachers and they will always take time out and go through things with you! (Parent of primary school pupil)

Parental involvement was particularly challenging in schools where a significant proportion of children entered school with 'below average ability in English vocabulary and experience'. A deputy headteacher spoke of how parental attitudes had changed under the early years of the headteacher:

There was a lot of work done ... to let them know what was required in the British system ... and there have been more parent governors from the community ... the English classes set up three years ago have been really successful in providing people with the idea that there is an opportunity to learn as adults. (Deputy headteacher of primary school)

One headteacher spoke of the need 'to be aware of the cultural and religious needs of the families' (Headteacher of primary school) for example, the difficulty of children who had to attend the Mosque for two hours each night in working at home.

A parent at the school spoke of 'the feeling' being right and the support for her on a death in the family. The challenge for this headteacher and others was, 'to get the parents into the understanding that education is for them and that it's a life long issue'. (Headteacher of primary school)

Community education was a recurring theme and all the heads were actively and directly involved:

He [the headteacher] tries to bring all aspects of the community to the school, and he's involved in lots of things in the community, and it never seems like too much trouble for him. (Parent of secondary school pupil)

The headteacher of this school was, 'passionate about schools preparing young people to make a difference in the community that they work in', and saw parents as, 'part of our team'; and he ensured regular feedback on the school through questionnaires and the school's website. According to one governor, the headteacher spent, 'a colossal amount of time with parents'.

It was about getting a real partnership going rather than a superficial one … I was very open, right from the start, that I was going to be very ambitious … I think that's taken eight years to get that message through to greater numbers than we used to do. The vast majority now understand where we're coming from and have jumped on board with us and have suddenly seen their children's aspirations rise considerably. (Headteacher of primary school)

Conclusion

These headteachers had successfully countered what Gleeson and Gunter (2001: 150) identify as, 'the endurance of structures that continue to limit … commitment to wider educational and participation enhancing values'. In these schools, 'interpersonal relations had not been supplanted by depersonalised or contrived forms of intimacy which produce new forms of self-regulation such as team work' (Blackmore, 1999: 137–8, in Gleeson and Gunter, 2001: 150). Rather, it was clear that they each had and were seen to have a strong sense of agency and moral purpose.

They had created in their schools their own reform agenda, what Smyth calls, 'educative restoration that constitutes the most likely antidote to the managerialist ideological onslaught' (Smyth, 2001: 128). Emboldened by their passion, each of the headteachers exercised commitment, care, collaboration, achievement, trust and inclusivity, and in doing so displayed both courage and persistence:

Such courage enables strategic non-compliance to take place in which priorities and decisions are made in accordance with ethical commitments to children and contextual factors around what can and cannot be realistically done. (Gleeson and Gunter, 2001: 152).

If someone says that he cares for some individual, community, or cause but is unwilling to risk harm or danger on his, her or its own behalf, he puts into question the genuineness of his care and concern. Courage, the capacity to risk, harm or damage oneself,

> *has its role in human life because of this connection with care and concern.* (MacIntyre, 1981: 192)
>
> For much of the time, headteachers work in situations which may reasonably be described as difficult, personally, emotionally and cognitively challenging, sometimes turbulent and occasionally violently disruptive. It requires intelligent passion to maintain a commitment over time, courage to persist in caring for every student in the class, those who are able, those who are not, those who are interested and those who are alienated. It takes intelligent passion to continue to believe in and be actively engaged in one's moral purposes and not to default under pressures of effort and energy. It takes intelligent passion not to be discouraged when school practices must be changed, new curricula absorbed, new rules of conduct met which seem to emphasize managerialism and bureaucracy at the expense of teaching. Leading well, over time, is a struggle and it takes intelligence and passion to continue to encourage self and others to lead and learn in changing and challenging times.

Note

[1] This chapter draws significantly upon 'The passion of successful leadership' by the author, published first in *School Leadership and Management*, 2004, 24(4): 425–37.

References

Blackmore, J. (1999) *Troubling Women: Feminism, Leadership and Educational Change*. Buckingham: Open University Press.

Day, C. and Leithwood, K. (2007) *Successful Principal Leadership in Times of Change: An International Perspective*. Dordrecht: Springer.

Day, C. (2005) 'Principals who sustain success: Making a difference in schools in challenging circumstances', *International Journal of Leadership in Education*, 8(4): 273–90.

Day, C.W. (2004) *A Passion for Teaching*. London: Falmer.

Fletcher-Campbell, F. (1995) 'Caring about Caring?', *Pastoral Care*, 9(1): pp. 26–8.

Fried, R.L. (1995) *The Passionate Teacher: A Practical Guide*. Boston, MA: Beacon Press.

Gleeson, D. and Gunter, H. (2001) 'The Performing school and the modernisation of teachers', in D. Gleeson and C. Husbands (eds) *The Performing School*. London: Routledge/Falmer. pp. 139–58.

Hargreaves, A. (1994) *Changing Teachers, Changing Times: teachers' work and culture in the postmodern age*. London: Cassell.

Hargreaves, D. (1972) *Interpersonal Relations and Education*. London: Routledge and Kegan Paul Ltd.

MacIntyre, A. (1981) *After Virtue*. Notre Dame, IN: University of Notre Dame Press.

Nash, R. (1973) *Classrooms Observed*. London: Routledge and Kegan Paul.

Nias, J. (1996) 'Thinking about Feeling: the emotions in teaching', *Cambridge Journal of Education*, 26(3): 293–306.

Noddings, N. (1984) *Caring: A Feminine Approach to Ethics and Moral Education*. Berkley, CA: University of California Press.

OECD (2001a) *Report on Hungary/OECD Seminar on Managing Education for Lifelong Learning*, Budapest.

OECD (2001b) *New School Management Approaches*. Paris: OECD.

Oxford English Dictionary (2nd edn) (2003) edited by John Simpson and Edmund Weiner. Clarendon Press, ISBN 0-19-861186-2.

Palmer, P. (1995) *The Courage to Teach*. San Francisco, CA: Jossey-Bass.

Sachs, J. (2003) *The Activist Teaching Profession*. Buckingham: Open University Press.

Sennett, R. (1998) *The Corrosion of Character: The Personal Consequences of Work in the New Capitalism*. New York: W.W. Norton & Company Inc.

Smyth, J. (2001) *A culture of teaching under new management*, in D. Gleeson and C. Husbands (eds) (2001) *The Performing School*. London: Routledge/Falmer pp. 118–36.

Thomson, P. (2002) *Schooling the Rustbelt Kids: Making the difference in changing times*. Australia: Allen & Unwin.

Chapter 5

Passionate leadership in action

Brent Davies

What drives some leaders to take on challenging schools in disadvantaged areas with a previous record of educational underachievement? The Academy movement[1] in the UK, in its initial set of schools, placed Principals in areas of social deprivation with school underperformance, often with local political hostility and with extraordinary pressures and demands to succeed. Why would individuals take on this role and put themselves in such a challenging environment? To answer this question the chapter reports on a research project that seeks to understand the leadership passions and motivations of leaders who undertake these roles. This chapter does not involve itself in the political arena regarding Academies but considers the leaders in those organizations. The research focused on the initial Academies that were set up in areas of considerable social challenge and economic deprivation. The research was based on qualitative interviews with Principals. The researcher aimed to distance the research from the political debate about academies and to look at how leaders can transform education in areas of high challenge; as such the lessons of this passionate commitment to improvement and change can be seen to have a wider application. In interpreting the data from the interviews, the following five elements emerged as to what enabled them to transfer their passion for education and social justice into action.

The chapter looks at five characteristics of the Principals and reports that they:

- are passionate leaders – driven by the centrality of social justice and moral purpose;
- have an absolute passion for transformation of learning outcomes;
- have a passion for sustainability by balancing the operational and strategic;
- are passionate about creating a 'sense of place' for learning;
- consider passion to be useless unless Principals have the personal characteristics to stay the course!

Passionate leadership – the centrality of social justice and moral purpose

An overwhelming factor raised explicitly by all Principals was a personal belief that they wanted to improve the lives and life chances of children in less advantageous communities. They had a deep conviction that 'they could make a difference' and they had the self-confidence in their own ability to make that difference. This was born out of a sense of fairness and giving children an opportunity that they had been denied before. This was something that the Principals were 'passionate' about from a deep felt sense of moral purpose and a desire for social justice. It is what I will refer to as 'passionate leadership'. This value-based leadership was referred to by two Principals:

> ... the whole sense of social justice really appealed to me and I'd always chosen to work in schools which had these types of challenges, so I guess my predisposition is to work with these children, these communities to help make a difference.

> I saw it as the opportunity to make a real difference in working with children with challenging social and economically divided backgrounds.

This belief both in social justice and that transformation could be achieved is seen by one Principal as being critically important and motivating:

Having been a head in two other schools, I have always had a commitment to what I guess you could call righting the wrongs of the past and so this post gave me the opportunity to further develop the work I had done in turning around my previous two schools. This was really appealing, hugely energising for me to think it was possible and indeed really believe it was possible.

Creating opportunities for young people and challenging existing perspectives explains the passion of one Principal for change:

The predecessor of the school had lost the focus of why it was in the community. It wasn't in the community to be a babysitting service and to provide care; it was in the community to give these young people the best platform for their future life. It was about moving people into understanding and believing that we were going to be different and making sure they were confident that we could be different [and] to make the difference and quickly.

The deeply felt belief that existing patterns of provision had failed children and that the Academy movement was an opportunity for those Principals to make a difference to children's lives was a driving force with all the Principals. This was articulated by two Principals:

One of the things I say to children is, 'You know, I don't believe life's treated you fairly, you know you've got an unfair deal but I haven't got a pill for it and if I actually excuse you from doing homework, looking smart and achieving, all I'm doing is condemning you to have the rest of your life as unfair as well as the beginning of it.' I don't expect any differently for the children in this school than I do for my own children.

I want the children to have a fair chance in life and I want them to not be limited by their background and by their educational attainment to date. So that's really all about aspirations; I want the youngsters to really stretch and reach and I want staff that are going to unlock that. I passionately believe that these kids are fundamentally no different than any other kids and should be able to do it.

The research has shown, across all the interviews, a tremendous commitment by the leaders to use the opportunities that Academies offer to make a significant difference in the life chances of children. They were morally driven to overcome social disadvantage and give the children in their care a first class education. This was not a utopian aspiration but grounded in a sense of purpose and hard work that would build a school that would achieve this for their students.

Key Leadership Issue

The 'why take on the challenge' is a passion for social justice and the chance to give disadvantaged youngsters a better deal and is shared throughout the school.

An absolute passion for transformational leadership

The *raison d'être* of the Academies programme is to transform learning and educational opportunities in areas that previously had inadequate educational performance by bringing fresh ideas and educational success.

Styles and approaches of transformational leadership were evident in all the Academy Principals interviewed. Much of the academic research on this transformational leadership has been summarized by Leithwood (2005). He articulates school-wide factors such as setting directions, developing people and redesigning the organization. He also identifies individual factors such as charisma, inspirational leadership, consideration for individuals and providing an intellectually stimulating workplace. These factors were reflected in the leadership practices of the Principals. One significant factor in the interviews was that for many of the Principals this was their second or third headship. They brought to the new post the experience of working in previously challenging schools which they had contributed to turning around. A common response was that they had to use that previous experience of transforming a school over five years into transforming the new Academy over a much shorter period of time (often only one year or even less). This transformation focus is one in which learning, teaching and standards are the absolute priority. One Principal articulated the need for a constant focus on raising standards:

> *I've got some fantastic senior staff, very, very driven, very focused. We haven't kept our eye off the ball once; our eye is constantly on the ball of learning and teaching, raising standards.*

Transformation is a challenging process which was commented on by one Principal:

> *To transform this place was all about the management of change and moving people from either a state of conscious or unconscious incompetence to a position where they can be proud of what they do, have confidence in what they do. It is about raising expectations in the face of enormous challenge, sustained challenge that just does not seem to ever go away. Transforming things here is not a quick fix and so a lot of resilience on the part of everyone is required and that isn't something that will happen overnight and then you can just move on to the next thing. You have to keep people's spirit up and that is a huge drain on any leader but it has to be done – it's like you are the unofficial life blood of the organisation whilst it is being transformed.*

Transformation is not just about transforming teachers and students, it is about transforming the hopes and expectations of parents and the community. One principal saw this as:

> *... raising people's aspirations and their sights and saying 'there is a world out there and your children are very bright, they can get into higher education and jobs in well paid occupations'.*

Most significantly, transformation is about organizational culture:

> *You've got to do a lot of unlearning of people to get away from the bad habits that were leading to failure in the past. That takes a lot of time, a lot of talking and a lot of modelling. It has to be reflected in the way you do everything – in talking to parents, the way you talk to students in the corridors, how you are with the staff ... everyone needs to see how you want it to be done so they can feel secure in mirroring it. I can see many of the things we are changing here in*

words the staff say at meetings or when the children answer my questions. It's not like they are brainwashed, but they can see the point of it – the outcomes – and that it works for the better.

However, those changes have to be sustainable. One Principal expressed this as:

We do have to transform things but I'm not prepared to make trans-formational changes that aren't sustainable, so if that means at some point I have to say, 'well what I've done in the first round is, you know, the quick, fairly easy fixes that should have been in place a long time ago, but now the second phase is in more depth, much more sustainable for the school even after I have moved on', then that's what I'll do. I have to make sure that what we do now is sus-tainable and robust otherwise there is no real point to it for the kids or staff and it needs to be properly developed further on that basis.

Academies are established to deliver significant improvements in performance. This transformation is the central leadership driving force of all the Principals interviewed in the research project. All Principals recognized the importance of rapid change and improve-ment and realized that that was their foremost challenge and their own and their senior staff's positions depended on achieving those outcomes. However, it was clear that leaders in the Academies did not see this as being achieved by a series of 'quick fixes' but by fun-damental improvement in learning and organizational culture that was sustainable.

Key Leadership Issue

The central focus of change leadership is to mobilize the school and community to promote rapid and sustainable improvement.

A passion for sustainability by balancing the operational and strategic dimensions of leadership

Establishing Academies in areas of previous educational disadvan-tage and underperformance presents a challenge and expectation for improvement. This, combined with the enhanced political visibility, presents enormous pressure for rapid short-term improvement in results. This is an extreme pressure particularly felt by the Principals. At one level this can be an oppressive pressure as witnessed by one comment:

> *In my first year as the Academy Principal, the system made me fear for my job and I genuinely mean that. I really did believe that it was like a football manager, that if we didn't turn things around within those 12 months the gun was to my head.*

At another level, there is a danger of looking to short-term fixes and not building long-term sustainability into the school. Answering the question 'Can you be strategic when the short-term demands are so great?' is critical for the long-term success of schools. The balancing of operational leadership and strategic leadership is of fundamental importance. This was recognized by one Principal:

> *Getting the strategic and operational balance right is crucial. I think that was partly the problem with the predecessor school ... they were totally operational, they were so hands on that they couldn't actually formulate a plan and that's still something I'm having a problem with some of the staff from the old school. Some of them still don't understand that actually long-term planning will make us a better place than just being out in the corridor reacting. I have a separate strategic and a separate operational meeting now to really hammer home the difference and the importance so the staff can see it.*

The leadership dimension of focusing on the basics of school systems and operational frameworks to ensure consistent high-quality education clearly has to be a focus for leaders. However, that focus has to be set in the context of building longer-term sustainable capacity. Principals also commented that it is also motivating for staff if they can see that operational and short-term initiatives which they are enacting in the current year are contributing to longer-term goals and priorities. In many cases, it was re-motivating the staff of the predecessor school. The ability to see current activities playing a part in the longer-term vision for the school is an important factor in establishing wider leadership understanding throughout the school.

There is a concept of the 'life cycle' of a school. This is where previous 'poor' or underperformance goes through states from 'improving', to 'satisfactory', to 'good', to 'outstanding'. To move through the first stage of improving to satisfactory, there is a tendency to believe that a strong operational and organizational focus is needed. While this is correct it should not be seen in isolation from the later stages of 'good' and 'outstanding'. Davies (2006) uses the concept of 'sequential' and 'parallel' leaders. Sequential leaders undertake and complete the operational necessities of organizational development, and when they are in place and working, they move on to considering what strategic agendas need to be addressed. In brief, they do the operational before the strategic. Parallel leaders do both concurrently. They recognize the operational imperatives and get on and address them but at the same time they link them to the longer-term strategic objectives of the school. They use the strategic objectives as a template to develop and asses the operational activities. A Principal recognized the life cycle stages of improvement as follows:

Well I think that's where the strategic bit comes in because when you're getting from unsatisfactory or inadequate to satisfactory, while so much is at this operations and systems level you have also to build strategic foundations. When you start moving from satisfactory to good and good to outstanding you've got to be so strategic and build on those foundations.

The challenge of finding time to do both the strategic and operational was articulated by another Principal:

I see myself being much more like the Chief Executive, that is the route we're going down and I think once the school is established that will run really well but at the moment it's still doing a lot of the operational stuff. It's almost like you do the operational stuff during the day and then you go home at weekends or holidays and do the strategic stuff, I have two jobs.

The leadership challenge of concurrently working on the operational imperatives while building a secure and sustainable strategic future recurred in the research interviews as a leadership issue that was fundamental to sustainable improvement.

Passionate about creating a 'sense of place' for learning

It is often said that it is easy to be successful with a new start in a new buildings but that is a very partial view. Several Academies have started in existing or temporary accommodation and have established a new organizational and learning culture before moving into new buildings. The reality is that a combination of the physical and organizational environment come together to create a 'sense of place' that reengineers both the organizational culture and the physical structure of the school. All the principals, while recognizing the importance of new physical surroundings, stressed the change in organizational culture as being more significant. A very telling account of this by one Principal was:

> *When you drive in the gate here the building and the grounds tell you what the culture is and as soon as the parent drives in/walks in they know the culture is one of quietude, calm, discipline, well dressed, well spoken, hard work, and that's where it starts, that's the ethos. So that everybody behaves themselves effectively in that calm, respectful of people to people and I mean everybody. That's students, staff, all employees, all parents, all visitors, everybody and if anybody steps out of line of that quietude that I wanted to create here, then they're gently reminded that this is a requirement of them.*

This change in culture is also about linking the wider community and providing for them as shown by this comment:

> *I feel as though we have mobilized a whole section of the community. There's just so much for them to do here from parenting classes, sports clubs, learning English and other languages and even cookery classes. It was a long time in coming but now we hand out as many*

application forms for student admissions to these people as we do membership of the fitness club here and our first choice applications for September have almost doubled. They all bring their friends to use the facilities and their friends want their children to go to school with each other so there are strong bonds too.

This change in culture is also about empowering staff to take ownership of their school and take responsibility for its success, as witnessed by this powerful response:

I remember one of the Heads of faculty saying at a meeting we had … 'when we move into the new building we've done all this preparation work together and it's our building, our school and we decide how it's organised, you know, we the teaching staff', and they do lead their own areas, they run their subject floors, they have taken control of their areas and they mirror what we do throughout the school so it's consistent all the way throughout wherever you are. We built that up together which is great. There's a massive huge, team spirit.

This change in culture is facilitated by the sponsors of the Academy who can bring a number of assets and attributes. One Principal describes how their sponsor brings an external view and powerful links and support as follows:

My sponsor brings to the Academy an outward looking perspective and a confident expectation that what he does can and should succeed. There is a genuine hunger and an expectation for success. This is what these kinds of people are used to in business which is why they are so successful themselves. They know you can't do it on your own so they look to get good people on the governing body to help and contribute so, you know, we've got significant people from the world of sport and the arts as well as people with serious business and project management experience and I learn from all of this and have become more entrepreneurial in my approach as a result.

Of course new buildings are very important in changing the surrounding learning fabric of the school. The building can be the physical representation of the changing learning culture of the school, as represented by these two observations:

But what I think this building has done in terms of transforming learning is made a statement about how important learning is. Secondly I'm absolutely certain it has done a lot about this concept of creating the partnership between adult and child because it is so open, adults and young people are working together, you know there's no such thing as hidden away staff areas and all this stuff, so I think that's been powerful. And I just think, yes, it's lifted spirits.

On the plus side we have created a much more open learning environment, you know every room is open to the building. So as you walk around you see in every classroom, every office, every work room, conference room, everything has a glass panel that you look into, there's no corridors so there's no hiding away, nothing ... everything's seen.

Creating a 'sense of place' combines the buildings, the organizational culture and the external relationship coming together to put learning at the head of the agenda. The combination of these factors creates the necessary conditions for transformation to take place.

Key Leadership Issue

Reengineer the organizational culture and the physical surroundings to create a 'sense of place' where learning can flourish.

Passion is useless unless Principals have the personal characteristics to stay the course

While there are many personal characteristics that these Principals display, four that were very evident in the research interviews were: personal resilience, positive mindset, ability to manage conflict, and risk taking. One further characteristic that emerged was the struggle to achieve a work–life balance.

The Principals report the pressures that come from hostility to the Academy movement and the intense scrutiny in the press. This is combined with the necessity of having to engage in very rapid change with significant consequences requires them to have considerable *personal resilience*. Thus resilience and strength of character and determination to deliver successful outcomes, amidst considerable pressures and challenges, seems to be a prerequisite for leading a successful school. As one leader put it:

> *Principals have got to have incredible self-confidence and belief in what they are doing and in their vision for what they want to see achieved. They have to have a lot of drive and a real sense of purpose about what they're doing. I think that confidence has to extend to be able to do some of the things that are not pleasant to do and actually have the confidence that it's the right thing. I learnt that in my first headship and it was much harder then but second time round I know what has to be done and why and therefore it is easier, if that's the right word. It is easier because I know that the final outcomes will be better for everyone.*
>
> *Well you haven't got to 'get down'. That's the hard bit because things do affect you. When I'm talking about this to other groups of people I tend to say do not to let the emotional highs and lows get to you, so you don't rejoice too much when you win a victory and you don't get suicidal when you lose a battle, but you just keep this sort of middle calm course whatever happens and that's a lot, lot easier to say than to do. I support my Vice Principals about this because I think when you're younger, you do tend to get the emotional highs and lows and you do go home and have sleepless nights thinking 'oh that's a failure'.*

This of course links to having a *positive mindset* and seeing opportunities and not just problems. Creating a 'can do' culture that tackles problems and seeks solutions was seen by many principals as one of the key ways of changing previous underperformance which resigned itself to accepting existing ways of doing things. Two of the Principals articulated this as:

> *At the school the glass is always half full, it's never half empty and that's the way you should approach things. But yes people say that when I speak and things at conferences or whatever, I'm very passionate about my school.*

You have to believe that you can make a difference, you have to believe that change is possible and some of the LA advisory people who've been working with us said when they came in last term that they've noticed a difference, they said the staff have stopped blaming the kids. I think if you start from the belief that every kid has talent and that every kid can achieve whatever, then you are an optimist and to me that's what education is about.

Clearly, taking over a previously unsuccessful school and creating a new school does involve the Principal in challenging previous levels of underperformance and establishing new expectations. The significant expectation for rapid change and improvement also creates pressure to change quickly. In such circumstance there is often conflict. The ability to *manage conflict* was reflected on by these Principals:

Do I find conflict easy? I have no problem deciding that somebody, by whatever means, has to leave us, that doesn't pose me a problem at all and I won't lose any sleep over that whatsoever. I might lose sleep over how I'm going to deal with it but the decision is made and that's what we've got to do and I have no problem going through with it.

You've got to take the conflict, you've got to not get too personal or involved in the conflict and you've got to de-personalise it, realise it's not directed at you but perhaps at you as the figurehead or whatever. You've got to try to empathise with people's personal situations because they might be very different from yours.

It is important to see risk taking not as a reckless activity but one where new and innovative practices are tried out and monitored to see if they add significant benefit to the school. With the opportunity of a new school and a new start, one Principal saw this as an opportunity not to be missed in the following words:

You only get one chance to make the really big first impression. You can always go back to something more traditional but you'll never get this chance again to just be so fundamentally radical.

The importance of decision-making being based on judgement and information before a risk is undertaken was highlighted by one Principal:

> *I don't do things unless I've got data. And you can get data very quickly, you can make risky decisions within 24 hours if you want to but I tend to sort of watch, listen, feel and then take a risk.*

The personal risk of taking on an Academy was highlighted by two Principals:

> *It is very high risk, it is very high risk and I'm being honest, I might not have done it if I'd been younger you know.*

> *Coming here yes, if it wasn't going to succeed under my leadership I knew perfectly well that another leader would be brought in.*

The enormous pressures of starting a new school was reflected in the long hours Principals spent during the day and at weekends at the school, especially in the first two years of the school's existence. This early pressure on work–life balance was reported by two Principals:

> *The hours that I worked in the first year were ... well they would have been untenable if they'd have carried on like that.*

> *During the transition phase, with everything that was happening, it just seemed to be 24/7. I really did spend a lot of time, probably too much time, in meeting community groups because what we were doing was having to convince local people that this was not the privatisation of state education, and I did 148 meetings in the first year.*

However, this early pressure does seem to shift:

> *I think it's definitely changed, the first year of a school like this where nothing is in place ... it was just crazy. I mean you didn't get a single weekend, you worked right the way through the summer. But now I actually do get weekends. Then you're actually better ... you're*

better for your staff you know because you've had a decent weekend.

Protecting the work–life balance of staff was also seen as very important:

I'll say, 'it's Friday, you've got lives, you've got families, get off home,' and then I'll go around the place and try and evict them. I mean how ridiculous. So I'm going around at sort of 4–4:30 saying 'go home' you know. 'Yes it is important to finish that but go home.'

Key Leadership Issue

Developing intra-personal skills is a vital factor in successful school leadership.

Conclusion

This piece of qualitative research has used the 'leadership voices' of Academy Principals to understand their passion for taking on challenging roles to transform the life of children. In summary, these passionate leadership issues were to:

- Make sure the 'why take on the challenge' is a passion for social justice and the chance to give disadvantaged youngsters a better deal and is shared throughout the school.
- Ensure that the central focus of leadership is to mobilize the school and community to promote rapid and sustainable improvement.
- Deliver rapid short-term improvement and at the same time create sustainable strategic development.
- Re-engineer the organizational culture and the physical surroundings to create a 'sense of place' where learning can flourish.
- Enhance intra-personal skills to create successful leadership.

The danger of this type of research is that it is dismissed because of political perspectives about Academies. If, however, a more balanced view is taken, the leadership dimensions of attempting radical transformation can provide insights from which we can learn and apply across the system.

Note

1 Academies are all-ability schools established by sponsors from business, faith or voluntary groups working in highly innovative partnerships with central Government and local education partners. Sponsors and the Department for Children, Schools and Families (DCSF) provide the majority of the capital costs for the Academy. Running costs are met in full by the DCFS. The Academies programme aims to challenge the culture of educational under-attainment and to deliver real improvements in standards. All Academies are located in areas of disadvantage. They either replace one or more existing schools facing challenging circumstances or are established where there is a need for additional school places.

References

Davies, B. (2006) *Leading the Strategically Focused School*. London: Sage.
Leithwood, K. and Jantzi, D. (2005) 'Transformational Leadership', in Davies, B. *Essentials of School Leadership*. London: Sage.

Acknowledgement

Thanks go to the Specialist Schools and Academies Trust to replicate research material here and in particular to Lesley King for her inspiration and educational passion.

Passionate leadership – schools and teachers

Chapter 6

Not so much a passion, more a way of life

John MacBeath

Passionate leadership is not easy to pinpoint within the pressured environment of schools driven by targets and performance tables. In many schools, passion is expressed only in the negative, a shared and strong antipathy to an oppressive environment in which the excitement of learning has been buried beneath layers of prescriptive policies. Yet it can be found if one looks beyond the obvious places and beyond conventional notions of leadership as performed at the apex of the organizational pyramid. This chapter argues that there is an intrinsic passion for learning which schools generally fail to sustain and that leadership may be similarly discouraged by the conventions and inhibitions of schooling. However, on a more optimistic note, passionate leadership may be found in many places. It tends to be informally dispersed rather than formally distributed, exercised in the very best schools more as a way of life than as a trait of charismatic individuals infusing everyone around with their singular vision.

The word 'passion' is not one that has immediate associations with school. Nor, in many people's minds would it be viewed as an apt descriptor for a headteacher or school principal. The images of the archetypical 'headmaster' of children's books and comics, lent further substance by the *Harry Potter* sagas, shape the popular imagination. These are not pure fiction, however, as they clearly resonate with people's experience of school in which passion may often have been expressed but rarely in the formal life of the school and rarely in encounters with the head. In the history of schooling, whatever happened to passion, and was there ever a golden era when it was actually admitted through the school gates?

A passion for learning

Human beings enter the world with a passion for learning. It is in their genes and ignited by an environment rich in possibilities. Learning is spontaneous, exploratory, driven from within and curbed only by limits put on it by protective adults and by the painful lessons of self-discovery. Exceptional children and young people are able to keep that passion alive through their school years, often with a little help from their friends, but most experience a slow process of attrition as learning becomes annexed by the strictures of schooling. Passion is lowly extinguished as much by rewards as by deterrents, by marks and grades, targets, competition, failure and a growing sense of inadequacy and diminished self worth. It is, as Jerry Starratt (2005: 3) describes it, a moral issue.

The learning agenda of the school must connect to the central moral agenda of the learners during their thirteen or more years in school, namely the agenda of finding and choosing and fashioning themselves as individuals and as a human community. As human beings they are searching, and must search for the truth of who they are. Educators miss this connection because they are accustomed to view the learning agenda of the school as an end in itself, rather than as a means for the moral and intellectual 'filling out' of learners as human beings. Schools assume that their learning agenda stands above and outside of the personal and civic life of learners. By and large the message communicated to learners is: leave your personal and civic lives at the schoolhouse door – certainly at the classroom door.

As with the nature of learning, lessons about leadership are also learned early. School is a place of few leaders and many followers and passion is something to be left at the front gate. In ten to 12 years of schooling it is remarkable how little we take away with us from the 15,000 hours of exposure to the curriculum, but we learn indelible lessons about relationships, about dualities and paradoxes – discipline and punishment, impulse and control, compliance and subversion.

There may be little scope for the exercise of leadership in the ritual life of the school but there is much to be learned, often painfully, in the underlife of school where passion finds an outlet and the nature of the world, winners and losers, becomes daily more clear. In Marshall McLuhan's (1965) terminology 'the medium is the message'.

In casual conversation or formal interviews with leaders in schools, universities, local government and community it is striking how much reference back there is to school years, to teachers, to classmates, (some now wives, husbands or partners), to critical incidents and defining moments. School, a society in miniature, models the world for us and while shaping the child, indelibly shapes the child in the adult.

The school effect

Is all of this to lay too much blame or credit at the door of schooling? Four decades of school effectiveness research has consistently shown that school effects are minimal by comparison with the influence of parents, family and neighbourhood, even though leadership recurs as a constant theme in virtually all of these studies (for example, Sammons et al., 1994). The titles of effectiveness literature following major studies – *Schools Make a difference* (Brookover, 1979) and *School Matters* (Mortimore et al., 1985) – reveal the need to reassert the importance of schooling in the wake of rhetorical onslaughts claiming that *School is Dead* (Reimer, 1971) or that school is 'a gap in your education' (Illich, 1971).

While the importance of leadership has been a recurring refrain, particularly in school effectiveness studies, the nature of leadership that could re-ignite learning has remained tantalizingly elusive. Indeed the potential of leadership to affect the deterministic impact of family, neighbourhood and peer group has been shown to be marginal (see for example, MacBeath et al., 2007). Another, more telling strand in effectiveness studies was the identification of the 'compositional' (or contextual) effect. This referred to the finding that the school, the curriculum, teachers and senior leaders were of less significance than whom you went to school with. This is the substance of Martin Thrupp's (1999) empirical work, illustrating the critical impact of the 'social mix'.

The social mix, or peer group effect, receives strong endorsement from Judith Harris's prize winning book *The Nurture Assumption* (1998) in which she offers evidence to challenge the assumption that it is parents or teachers who are the primary shapers of dispositions and aspirations. Expression of adolescent passions are reserved for the intimacy and trust of peer group forums where leadership is expressed in the interplay of authority and influence.

School failure and lack of leadership are intimately conjoined in the minds of policy makers. School failure is defined in terms of low student attainment and leadership in terms of strong individuals able to turn a school round. An alternative proposition is that where schools fail is in their ability to harness the passion of pupils that defaults into subversive outlets. It is underpinned by a conception of leadership which ignores or constrains what Soo Hoo (1993) describes as the 'treasure within' – the inherent capacity of young people for passionate leadership.

While media are fond of headlining the excesses of today's youth, (a complaint of Socrates some years earlier), there is also among the young an idealism and desire for a better world that is sometimes allowed expression in schools. Their initiative, creative capacity and commitment almost always seems to come as a surprise to their teachers.

We seek the holy grail 'out there' and we ignore the latent talent within, often mute and inglorious because it has never been given the opportunity to grow and flourish. In response to the widespread perception of a 'recruitment crisis' (MacBeath, 2006) Mckinsey advocated a 'war for talent' (Michaels et al., 2001). It was premised on the assumption that the talent existed somewhere else and had to be found and captured to affect institutional change. The inadequacy of aggressive recruitment, premised on the maxim that, 'talented leaders create great organisations', lay in its failure to recognize the limiting conception of what talent is and where it resides. Malcolm Gladwell's (2002) rejoinder was 'great organisations create talented leaders'.

The McKinsey 'war' was set in a context of a recruitment and retention 'crisis' in which there is a growing reluctance for teachers to apply for headship/principalship largely because the job is seen as too stressful, too thankless and too inimical to work–life balance. These perceptions of teachers derive largely from what they see of their own senior leaders, while the system as a whole witnesses a progressive erosion of talent as a range of contextual factors working together to diminish energy and creativity, blunting any residual passion for the task. It is a futile pursuit therefore to seek out talent if the problem lies within. If systems and organizations are able to destroy talent, might they, with a different set of prevailing conditions, also be able to create it?

While the McKinsey thesis is premised on the qualities of the individual, the Gladwell thesis looks to the organizational context. Seeing things through this latter lens carries with it no presumption that headteachers and senior leaders need to be demonstrably passionate people, wearing their emotions on their sleeves, drowning others with their exuberance and single-minded commitment. Indeed passionate leadership may be expressed in what Greenleaf (1997) referred to as 'servant leadership', a self-effacing desire to be of service to others. In Collins's (2001) seminal, and much quoted, study *Good to Great*, the corporate leaders singled out for praise were often surprised to be so honoured. Some of Collins's leaders were quiet, unassuming, modest people. Their passion expressed itself in the people they appointed and whose passion they nourished. It was manifested in their hopes and dreams for their organizations.

The hidden passion: teachers as learners and leaders

Teachers have learned to keep their emotions in check and to divorce their personal lives from their professional lives. They are taught early 'never punish in anger' and they must learn to be rational and judicious in their responses no matter what the provocation. The following anecdote had a profound impression on some of my own students who referred to it as a defining moment many years later after they had become heads of department and headteachers.

In a seminar group graduate students in pre-service training were sharing dilemmas they encountered in their school placements – how to respond to overtly sexual remarks, to bad language, to provocation, testing the limits of the new teachers' tolerance and limited repertoire of available sanctions. I replied to one student's account of a dilemma by saying 'Only punish in anger', quoting Sanderson, the famous headmaster of Oundle School. I was immediately corrected by another student – 'You mean never punish in anger'. Others smiled at my apparent mistake. I asked them to reflect for a moment on the idea. There was a long silence and some shook their heads and said nothing. Some seemed to be trying to come to terms with the notion. Gradually, however, the discussion took us into complex territory – how to respond to a deeply offensive remark, disrespect for a fellow pupil, a racist slur. Some were willing to agree that, while not punishment in a strict sense, to show anger at what you find personally offensive could carry much more weight and meaning than a dispassionate response pronounced from a position of authority.

The early years of teaching are a struggle for identity and the dilemma of what it means to be a 'professional'. Some of the most penetrating insights on that struggle are contained in Kevin Ryan's book *Don't Smile Until Christmas* in which the contained passion in the classroom conveys a picture of an incipient time bomb ready to explode if the teacher does not don the mask of authority and establish the rules of order from day one. For many teachers the question of identity is left behind, their professional role held in place both by formal conventions of schooling and by the informal norms of colleagues. Numerous research studies (for example, Little, 1995, Smylie and Denny, 1990) have illustrated the power of 'the way we do things round here', locking new teachers into perceptions of self that become cemented over time.

This issue appears to be global in nature, a consequence of competitive policy pressures in which teachers are cast in the delivery role. Data from the Organisation for Economic Co-operation and Development (OECD), Trends in International Mathematics and Science Study (TIMSS) and the European Commission has provoked a widespread urgency (some might say moral panic) among policy makers. Comparisons among countries have set the stage and provide the script for the players, impacting with equal force in North America, Europe, Australasia and Asia. In Taiwan, for example, Pam and Yu (1999: 82) report:

At present teachers seem to be in a passive position when facing the reform proposals. They feel that they are the subjects to be reformed rather than being the change agents.

Katzenmeyer and Moller's book *Awakening the Sleeping Giant* (2001) was subtitled, *Helping Teachers Develop as Leaders*, preceding the fashion for 'distributed leadership' but arguing, with passion, for a recognition of incipient leadership of teachers and for the link to be made between professional autonomy, the sharing of power and professional learning communities.

As Broadhead et al. (1999) have argued, if teachers are to be held accountable as agents of change, accountability needs to be matched by responsibility.

> *The class teacher is the ultimate gatekeeper in relation to change; perhaps the time has come to enable them to be at the forefront of change, rather than what seems evident at the present time, at the end of a long chain of responsibility passing.* (p. 25)

Teachers at the forefront of change is an idea that sits uneasily within increasingly top down mangerialist cultures and the growing institutional power distance between those who lead and those who follow. In the United States, Ann Liebermann has written extensively about the clash between teachers who aspire to lead and the bureaucratic norms of their schools. She found that, in addition to (or as a concomitant of) pressure from above, strong teacher norms of egalitarianism in the teacher culture inhibited anyone from sticking their neck out too far, exercising leadership without formal invitation or sanction. In the writing projects which she initiated, the dormant qualities of leadership suddenly found expression. Lieberman and Friedrich (2007) describe teachers who discovered a long buried passion. Two teachers, Austen and Liz, re-ignited their desire to do something to address issues of gender and race respectively, their 'burning passion' for the cause leading them to devise a number of strategies in their own classrooms and to build alliances that became the impetus for change within their schools. Austen first established the girls' after school writing club and then worked behind the scenes to establish single gender classrooms inside her school. Liz engaged her students in studying the history of their own school which led to broader political activism using writing to improve the physical condition of her own school as well as that of other DC schools.

For others, discovery of the leader within came as a shock:

> *... I had never presented anything to other adults at all, except in*
> *church kinds of settings, but not in a school setting. But the idea that*
> *I might have some sort of professional development to share with*
> *other teachers had never occurred to me before the writing project.*
> (Shayne Goodrum, Focus Group, June 2006)

The shock of self discovery finds a close parallel in Italy where, in a similar summer school, the question voiced by teachers was 'what sort of leader can *I* be?' Brotto and Barzano report:

> *One of the participants, Stefania, makes a distinction between* 'stare
> con' *('being with') and* 'essere per' *('being for'), her aspiration for*
> *leadership seen as 'being with', marked by 'contagious' listening,*
> *empathy, teamwork and sense-making, allied with 'being for' as*
> *mutual empowerment and service.*

These have the making of what Richard Elmore (2005) describes as internal accountability in which the leadership culture is one that precedes and shapes the response of the schools to policy pressures that are outside the organization. The level or degree of internal accountability is measured by the degree of convergence among what individuals say they are responsible for (responsibility), what people say the organization is responsible for (expectations), and the internal norms and processes by which people literally account for their work (accountability structures). Elmore concludes that with strong internal accountability schools are likely to be more responsive to external pressure for performance. Evaluating accountability in a Canadian context, Ben Jafaar (2006) described a hybrid model of economic bureaucratic accountability and ethical professional accountability living side by side which can be resolved within the school through by what she terms 'inquiry-based accountability'. This treats all forms of external mandate, evaluation or inspection as entry points for professional discussions about learning experiences, opportunities and outcomes, directing people's attention to the real priorities for the young people that schools are intended to serve.

The hidden passion: pupils as learners and leaders

Opening the 1997 Thinking Skills Conference in Singapore the Prime Minister Tony Blair, laid out a vision for education in his country, already well positioned in the international performance tables but an achievement, as he saw it, devoid of 'fire'.

> *What is critical is that we fire in our students a passion for learning, instead of studying for the sake of getting good grades in their examinations. Their knowledge will be fragile, no matter how many As they get ... It is the capacity to learn that will define excellence in the future not simply what young people achieve in school.*

It is a vision which finds similar expression in many countries of the Asia–Pacific Rim, in Shanghai and Hong-Kong (Lo, 1999) and in Japan where individuality, creativity and *ikuru-chikara* (ability to survive in a changing society) are seen as high priority goals (Fujita and Suk-ying, 1999). To 'fire the passion' in Goh Chok Tong's (1997) words, is most likely to be realized when there is an embrace of servant leadership. It may be an odious notion to self important leaders but if the leadership of pupils is a genuinely held ambition, attention needs to be paid to the conditions within which pupil leadership can find expression. There is no better example of servant leadership and passionate pupil leadership in the contemporary history of schooling than the confrontation in the Royal Courts of Justice between Summerhill pupils and the combined might of the DfES and Ofsted. After three days of trial and a capitulation from the government side, Zoe Readhead, the school principal, was offered a compromise on Ofsted's demands. She replied that it was not her decision to accept the conditions of the government climb down, so for over an hour three pupils took their place on the judge's bench and debated the conditions under which they would accept the government's offer with regard to inspection, compulsory lessons and separate toilets.

What might easily be perceived as an abdication of authority on the headteacher's part was in fact a celebration of the authority of the young and their capacity for wise and well balanced judgement, honed in the training ground of a 'school' in which it is the whole community of adults and children which sets the limits and establishes the norms. Pupil leadership in Summerhill is cultivated systematically through giving pupils responsibility to chair meetings of the teaching, support and caretaking staff as well as all the pupils. These twice-weekly meetings vividly illustrate the capacity of children and young people to rise to the occasion and the capacity of teachers and the headteacher to practise followership. The trust this entails in pupils' ability to exercise responsible judgement is rarely disappointed.

Such practice can only be understood within the particular context that is Summerhill, and attempts to replicate its democratic government and *laissez-faire* approach to attendance at classes have run aground on the inherent contradictions within a hierarchical and highly prescriptive state system. Within the main stream of schooling the challenge for senior leaders is to the latitude for children and young people to lead, and even sometimes to lead with passion.

In the rush through the curriculum to satisfy the test teachers struggle to find any wiggle room for spontaneous excitement or surprise. In recognition of the tightly defined curriculum and assessment pathway, schools have increasingly looked to more open 'extra' curricular spaces in which leadership and learning may be engaged. The context for these is offered through sports, clubs, orchestras and choirs, drama, school plays, community events and variegated forms of study support in libraries, youth facilities and football clubs and residential weekends. An evaluation of study support – an umbrella term for all out-of-school-hours activities – (MacBeath et al., 2001) provided numerous exemplars of erstwhile passive, seat bound, disaffected young people awakening dormant qualities of leadership and a passion for achievement.

While taking initiative, leading teams, helping and directing others tends not to be seen by young people as 'leadership', members of staff need to be alert to the significance of the incipient activities that can help to capture and celebrate the leadership moment and bring these in from the cold, into the heart of the school's and classroom's daily business.

One of the more successful attempts to bring children and young people more into the leadership discourse is at times of appointment of a new headteacher. While in some schools this may be no more than a tokenistic gesture, in others it has often proved highly revealing, illustrating what children see that adults don't see. Where adults tend to look for the power of logic and argument, children tend to read more into the emotional content. Some of the things pupils have told us are that they respond to eye contact, adults who turn towards them when speaking, addressing them directly rather than addressing the panel, listening to them sensitively and accurately and showing an ability to share a joke. Primary age children, given free reign, rather than following pre-prepared and teacher-led prompts, ask about personal lives such as the applicant's children, pets, holidays, likes and dislikes. These may seem trivial from an adult perspective and may draw indulgent smiles but children are much more at home in the personal and emotional arena than are their teachers. Although few schools would risk accepting young people as the final arbiter, senior staff attest to having had their eyes opened to unsuspected qualities of a candidate, and been led in a real sense by the insights of their students.

The term 'pupil voice' has entered the vocabulary in the last decade or so but covers a multitude of interpretation, including the ritualistic gathering of survey data and token consultation. There is an attendant danger in romanticizing pupil voice and, in the process, diminishing opportunities to hear the teacher voice which may be equally silenced by structural conventions insulated to the acoustic of school, unable to tune in to the bandwidth through which differing voices carry (Moos, 2003). If student voice is to be understood, it is only by grasping the complexity of voices which find, or are denied, expression within the organizational life of schools. Schools are places in which voices carry, and carry in differing bandwidths. There are voices which demand to be listened to by virtue of their status. Some are strident voices while others speak softly but with inherent authority. Over the years, teachers', students' and parents' voices have been silenced by rules, by conventions and *mores* and by the weight of historical inertia. Nor do students or teachers speak with one voice but it is in the counter weight and balance of the school acoustic that cultures thrive or wither.

Honest attempts to tune into pupils' concerns recognize where command, consultation and decision-making are more or less appropriate. The Danish scholar Per Schultz Jorgensen's ladder of participation (Figure 6.1) provides a useful framework for school staff and/or pupils to reflect on current practice and to consider what kinds of decision-making are appropriate for different purposes and the extent to which some might assume a higher position on the ladder.

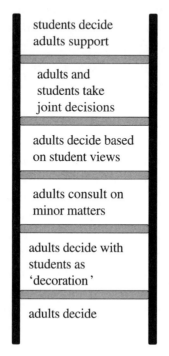

students decide
adults support

adults and
students take
joint decisions

adults decide based
on student views

adults consult on
minor matters

adults decide with
students as
'decoration'

adults decide

Figure 6.1: *The ladder of participation* (Schultz Jorgensen, 2003)

The Learning School

Exemplifying the highest rung in the ladder is the Learning School, now in its ninth year of operation. The brainchild of an assistant headteacher in Anderson High School on Shetland, it illustrates not only risk taking of a very high order but one repaid 'in spades'. In 1998, school students from a number of different countries were invited to take a gap year from their studies to conduct a global self-evaluation project. The plan was for them as a group to spend four to six weeks in each of six different schools in South Africa, Sweden, Scotland, Japan, Korea and the Czech Republic as visiting researchers, working alongside fellow students and with classroom teachers to research learning and teaching. In each location these young people would live with host families, in most contexts without a common first language and, in some cases, with no common linguistic ground at all. By travelling around the world on a single ticket and living off the hospitality and goodwill of host families, project costs were projected to be minimal. Before embarking on their global adventure, students spent an intensive two weeks familiarizing themselves with research methods, developing the tools of their research, building the collaborative team leadership which would see then through nine months of travelling, living and working together in close proximity. Students were encouraged to keep weekly diaries, recording their personal reflections both on their work with schools and on their own developing thinking.

What these young people recorded in their diaries illustrated the intensity of the experience which they spoke of with unconcealed passion. As they describe the impact of these new and unfamiliar contexts, the impact on their learning is contrasted with their prior school experience.

> *I have probably learnt as much in these ten months as I did in 13 years of school.* (Jolene, in MacBeath and Sugimine, 2003: 38)

A Scottish student takes a retrospective view of the impact of learning beyond school and the test it has offered to his self-awareness and academic identity.

> *This year has been a massive education to us all, an almost vertical learning curve. I often worried that I was not using this opportunity to learn as much as I could but now after having stepped back indefinitely from this particular journey I can see how by watching and feeling another culture from within you cannot help but learn infinite amounts. It is the greatest educational tool ever to have at one's disposal. Teaching things schools will never be able to teach, through first hand experience, feeding a desire to understand the world in which we live. This year has given me a real thirst to continue to test myself academically and to become more aware of different societies, cultures and people, as I am sure it has to everyone who was a part of Learning School 2.* (Colin, in MacBeath and Sugimine, 2003: 36)

A 16-year-old Korean student, speaking emotionally at a Cambridge conference at the culmination of Learning School 3 described how for the first time he had found his own voice after ten years of school. Preoccupation with hard work, after hours cramming and swotting for exams, had left neither time nor incentive to think for himself or to question received wisdom from his teachers. The Korean researcher Sung-Sik Kim (2002) provides confirmatory evidence for the constraining effects of Korea's school system and casts his own country's national performance (second only to Finland in the 2002 PISA study) in a more critical light.

The continuous thread in the Learning School narrative is of individual lives lived in and through a kaleidoscope of sites, shifting daily from family to peer group to school classroom and back again, each new set of relationships requiring a different linguistic register and social protocol. And as the group uproots and moves every four to six weeks to new cultural contexts, *mores* and social boundaries have to be readjusted and relearned. In each situation, self-concept and self-efficacy are confronted by the novelty of the experience. The situations perceived as 'challenges' by the three students, required them to reframe their familiar self-conceptions and forced them to start a new form of negotiated identity. When they became comfortable with the new identities, the negotiation was settled although this proved to be a simply temporal respite, waiting for the next challenging situation to be encountered.

> *This year has allowed me to see things from a different angle and to realise that sometimes we place limitations on ourselves and that there is so much more that we can do.* (Jolene, in MacBeath and Sugimine, 2002: 38)

With a new meta-perspective on schooling, some found it hard to adjust to the passivity and intellectual constraints of school life and learning. Others, though, have been able to channel their energy into changing their schools. The best success story, perhaps, comes from Hong Kong where a student returned to his school with determination to implement a school-wide self-evaluation project. Galvanizing his peers and enlisting the support of his principal, he maintained the momentum of his learning, realized his own self-efficacy and put in place a mechanism for all students' voices to be heard. Karolina, a Swedish student in Learning School 2 said:

> *One thing that Learning School did for me and probably for everyone else that has done a similar thing is that it has opened the doors in my mind and I now believe that I can do anything. The question we all have to ask ourselves is, are we brave enough to jump out there to the unknown not knowing what we might find or would we rather stay on the safe grounds? One last word is, jump! It is only you who are holding yourself back. If you do not take the step out you might regret it for the rest of your life but if you do, you can always come back to safety again.* (MacBeath and Sugimine, 2002: 36)

Through this considerable body of evidence we are afforded insights into a process of self-realization and the emergence of new voices as these young people reflect on who they are and who they are becoming. The way in which the sense of self is affected through the transition from one site to the next is striking in its parallels with Weiss and Fine's collection of essays in their edited book *Construction Sites* (2000), which chronicles how young people construct meaning from their experience in differing situations and through the interplay of various sites.

The hidden passion: leaders as learners

Those who assume a leadership role do so for a variety of reasons. Where there is passion it may also derive from differing motives, for power, status, recognition, for the ability to effect change, or be driven by a quest to learn and to lead learning, Hesselbein defines great leaders in these terms:

> *The most notable trait of great leaders, certainly of great change leaders, however, is their quest for learning. They show an exceptional willingness to push themselves out of their own comfort zones, even after they have achieved a great deal. They continue to take risks, even when there is no obvious reason for them to do so. And they are open to people and ideas even at a time in life when they might reasonably think – because of their success – that they know everything.* (Hesselbein, et al., 1996: 78)

Exploring in an Australian context how leaders make decisions, Neil Dempster (2008) describes school principals as starting from a 'first impulse' or ethically intuitive position, sometimes experienced as 'gut' reactions, sometimes as a firm conviction arising spontaneously from the deep values that they hold as an individual. 'Other people do not always share the intuitions we find self-evident', he writes, arguing that the important attribute that principals, as final arbiters need, is the understanding that similar experiences are also true for their colleagues, and that one's own 'first impulse' should be tested in the light of how others see the situation. There is support for his stance from research showing that school leaders build trust and respect for their decisions when they enrol trusted and respected others during the decision-making process (Duignan, 2003).

While the 'first impulse' of the leader is put on hold while broader perspectives on the ethical issue are canvassed, writes Dempster, 'my analysis tells me that it is unlikely that an experienced principal will implement a decision with which he or she does not feel at personal ease. Without the decision feeling right, fair, just and good, it is too difficult to sleep soundly at night'.

The distinguishing mark of passionate leaders is that they breathe life and excitement into their schools. This is described by Sackney and Mitchell (2007: 87) as the essence of successful schools.

We have found that, in successful schools, learning leaders know the people, the organizations, the communities, and the contexts; they ask questions rather than provide answers; and they know what is happening with teaching and learning. Most importantly, they find ways to release the creative energy of teachers and students, for this is the force that fosters experimentation and that breathes life, excitement, and enthusiasm into the learning environment for students and for teachers. This implies, of course, that leaders are comfortable with ambiguity, that they are more interested in learning than in outcomes, and that they trust teachers and students to work their magic in the classrooms.

Michael Apple has argued that the academic world has to recognize that teachers work in increasingly intensified conditions and that this demands a form of enquiry and a form of support in which leaders, critical friends, university academics and others who work with teachers act as, 'story tellers and secretaries' enabling teachers' voices to be heard (Apple, 2006). The ability to listen and tune in to secret harmonies (Nias et al., 1989) as well as discordant notes is the hallmark of leadership which allows leadership activity to flow through the school and to grow from the ground up. When leadership is recast as activity – what people do and say rather than where they sit – this can be both disturbing and liberating for headteachers and others in positions of authority.

In 1971, Neil Postman and Charles Weingartner published a book that was symbolic of its time – *Teaching as a Subversive Activity*. It was a prescribed text in many faculties of education in which a rising generation of staff, nurtured on dissent and radical alternatives, hoped to inspire those entering the profession to be sceptical, to think for themselves and to do so with a passion. The Postman and Weingartner book was, perhaps disappointingly for some, not about political demonstration but about the nature of teaching and learning as essentially concerned with disturbing preconceptions and shaking up inert ideas. It was about asking the kinds of incisive questions that provoke thought and enquiry. Socrates had thought of it a few millennia before and in doing so proved just how powerful, and dangerous, thinking for yourself could be.

Where there is a passion the subversion generally follows because genuine passion has very little room for compromise. Caring deeply about learning carries with it a commitment, in Bennis and Nanus's (1985) words 'to do the right thing'. Subversive leadership aims at creating and recreating cultures in which people – teachers, students, support staff, volunteers and parents – ask questions. This may be framed as research, teacher-led enquiry, action learning enquiry or may be the very essence of classroom dialogue – 'meaning flowing through it' (Bohm, 1983). 'Hope fires a neuron in the brain', writes David Bohm. Hope and optimism have intellectual correlates. They inform reason and are informed by reason. Rather than seeing goals and targets, development planning, self evaluation and inspection as the dead hand of policy, for passionate leadership these all assume an emotional colour. Goals and targets are construed from what you believe in and care passionately about as a staff. Planning becomes living planning, an ongoing and dynamic process. Self-evaluation is an embedded and vibrant aspect of a school's daily life. Inspection provides a rare and welcome opportunity to tell the school's authentic story to a critical external audience. Passionate leadership is courageous leadership. And when expressed as shared and owned commitment by a school staff it can be perilously subversive of the established order. By the questions they ask shall ye know them. By the answers they are willing to accept shall you get to know them more fully.

Passion, while not always associated in the public mind with a moral impetus, in an educational context flows directly from a deep-seated belief about pedagogic purpose. It provides the article for faith for principle-led, shared, and passionate leadership – 'Here we stand we can do no other'.

References

Apple, M. (2006) *Markets, Standards, and Inequality.* Keynote Address to International Congress on School Effectiveness and Improvement (ICSEI). Fort Lauderdale, Florida, USA audio recording retrieved from the worldwide web on 10th March 2006 http://www.leadership. fau.edu/icsei2006/archive.htm

Ben Jaafar, S. (2006). 'From performance-based to inquiry-based accountability', *Brock Education, 16*(2): 62–77.

Bohm, David (1983) *Wholeness and the Implicate Order.* New York: Ark Paperbacks.

Broadhead, P., Cuckle, P. and Hodgson, J. (1999) 'Promoting pupil learning within a school development framework', *Research Papers in Education,* 14:3: 275–94.

Brookover, W. (1979). *School Social Systems and Student Achievement: Schools Can Make a Difference.* New York: Praeger.

Brotto, F. and Barzano, G. (2008) 'Leadership, learning and Italy: a tale of two atmospheres', in J. MacBeath and Y.C. Cheng *Leadership for Learning: international perspectives.* Rotterdam: Sense Publishers.

Collins, J. (2001) *Good to Great.* New York: HarperCollins.

Dempster, N. (2008) 'Leadership for Learning: Some Ethical Connections', in J. MacBeath and Y.C. Cheng (eds), *Leadership for Learning: international perspectives,* Rotterdam: Sense Publishers.

Duignan, P. (2003) 'Formation of capable, influential and authentic leaders for times of uncertainty', paper presented at the Australian

Principals' Association Conference, Adelaide: September.

Elmore, R. (2005) *Agency, Reciprocity, and Accountability in Democratic Education*. Boston, MA: Consortium for Policy Research in Education.

Fujita, H. and Suk-Ying, H. (1999) 'Postmodern restructuring of the knowledge base in Japanese mass education: Crisis of public culture and identity', *Education Journal*, 26(2): 37–53.

Gladwell, M. (2002) The talent myth: Are smart people overrated? *New Yorker*, 22 July, pp, 28–33.

Greenleaf, R. (1997) *Servant Leadership*. New York: Paulist Press.

Harris, J.R. (1998) *The Nurture Assumption*. London: Bloomsbury.

Hesselbein, F., Goldsmith, M., Beckard, R. and Drucker, P. (1996) *The Leader of The Future*. San Francisco, CA: Jossey-Bass.

Illich, I, (1971) *Deschooling Society*. London: Penguin.

Jorgensen, P.S. (2004) 'Children's Participation in a Democratic Learning Environment', in J. MacBeath and L. Moos *Democratic Learning: the challenge to school effectiveness*. London: Routledge.

Katzenmeyer, M. and Moller, G. (1996) *Awakening the Sleeping Giant*. Thousand Oaks, CA: Sage Publications Inc, Corwin Press.

Lieberman, A. and Friedrich, L. (2007) 'Changing Teachers from Within: Teachers as leaders', in J. MacBeath and Y.C. Cheng. *Leadership for Learning: international perspectives*. Amsterdam: Sense Publishers.

Lo, L.N.K. (1999) 'Knowledge, Education and Development in Hong Kong and Shanghai', *Education Journal*, 27(1): 55–91.

MacBeath, J., Gray, J., Cullen, J., Frost, D., Steward, S. and Swaffield, S. (2007) *Schools on the Edge: Responding to challenging circumstances*. London: Paul Chapman Publishing.

MacBeath, J. (2006) 'The Talent Enigma', *International Journal of Leadership in Education*, 9(3): 183–204.

MacBeath, J. and Sugimine, H. with G. Sutherland and M. Nishimura and students of the Learning School (2003) *Self-evaluation in the Global Classroom*. London: Routledge.

MacBeath, J., Kirwan, T. and Myers, K. (2001) *The impact of study support. A report of a longitudinal study into the impact of participation in out-of-school-hours learning on the academic attainment attitudes and school attendance of secondary school students*. Research Report RR273, DfES.

McLuhan, M. (1965) *Understanding Media*. London: McGraw Hill.

Michaels, E., Handfield-Jones, H. and Axelrod, B. (2001) *The War for Talent: How to Battle for Great People*. Boston, MA: Harvard Business School Press.

Moos, L. (2003): *Paedagogisk ledelse – om ledelsesopgaven og relationerne i uddannelsesinstitutioner.* København: Børsens Forlag. [Educational Leadership – on leadership's purpose and relationships in educational institutions].

Mortimore, P., Sammons, P., Stoll, L., Lewis, D. and Ecob, R. (1988) *School Matters: The Junior Years.* Somerset: Open Books and Berkeley, CA; University of California Press.

Nias, J., Southworth, G. and Yeomans, R. (1989), *Staff Relationships in the Primary School: A Study of Organisational Cultures.* London: Cassell.

Pan, H.L. and Yu, C. (1999) 'Educational reforms with their impacts on school effectiveness and school improvement in Taiwan, R.O.C.', in *School Effectiveness and School Improvement,* 10(1): 86–99.

Postman, N. and Weingartner, G. (1971) *Teaching as a subversive activity.* Harmondsworth: Penguin Books.

Reimer, E. (1971) *School is Dead.* Harmondsworth: Penguin.

Ryan, K. (1971) *Don't Smile Until Christmas: accounts of the first year of teaching.* Chicago, IL: University of Chicago Press.

Sackney, L. and Mitchell, C. (2007) 'Leadership for learning: A Canadian perspective', in J. MacBeath and Y.C. Cheng *Leadership for Learning: international perspectives.* Amsterdam: Sense Publishers.

Sammons, P. Hillman, J. and Mortimore, P. (1994) *Key Characteristics of Effective Schools: A Review of School Effectiveness Research.* London: Office of Standards in Education.

Smylie, M.A. and Denny, J.W. (1990) Teacher Leadership: Tensions and Ambiguities in Organizational Perspective, *Educational Administration Quarterly,* 26(3): 235–59.

Soo Hoo, S. (1993) 'Students as partners in research and restructuring schools', *The Educational Forum,* 57, Summer: 386–93.

Starratt, R.J. (2005) 'Cultivating the moral character of learning and teaching; a neglected dimension of educational leadership', *Journal of School Leadership and Management,* 25(4): 399–411.

Sung-Sik, Kim, (2002) 'The influence of private education on schooling in Korea: High academic achievement and "school collapse"', paper presented at the ICSEI 2002 Conference, Copenhagen, Denmark: 3–7.

Thrupp, M. (1999) *Schools Making a Difference: Let's Be Realistic.* Buckingham: Open University Press.

Weiss, L. and Fine, M. (2000) *Construction Sites: Excavating Race, Class and Gender Among Urban Youth.* New York: Teachers College Press.

Chapter 7

The emotional geographies of educational leadership

Andy Hargreaves

Emotion and reason

It is hard, indeed impossible, to imagine a world, our work, or even a simple thought without emotion. Without emotion we would have no capacity to change, to imagine and have feelings about the future, or to carry the implicit emotional bias that forces us to judge and enables us to plan without calculating all the endless rational options for choosing, far into eternity (Damasio, 1994; Schwartz, 2004). Without emotion, we would have no passions for causes or work to drive us, no sense of calling or vocation to guide us, and no greater purpose to sustain us in the face of setbacks and adversity. Without emotion, there would be no impulse or imperative for justice, as we would be unable to empathize with the suffering of others, or to experience the guilt that gives rise to restitution and reparation after we have mistreated or betrayed them.

Emotions colour our thoughts and animate our actions. Courage, choice and change are unimaginable without them. In his *Expression of Emotions in Man and Animals*, Charles Darwin (1965) points out that even 'reflection' is a human emotion, involving a furrowing of the brow that is now associated with intense concentration, but that first emerged when our ancestors shielded their eyes from the sun as they searched for game on the horizon.

Emotions, then, are an essential and inalienable part of all human action. We would not be human without them. But this does not mean that they are always a force for good. Emotions can arouse and inspire us to achieve higher ends but just as easily, they can overwhelm our better judgement. The emotional life can be jealous and vengeful, envious and avaricious, nostalgic and narcissistic, maudlin and mawkish – clouding our capacity to help those we serve. But equally, without emotion, we are not only lesser human beings, unable to change or judge or be more just, but we are not really human at all as we cannot imagine the future, act purposefully or interact effectively with others. Human life is emotional life, strong and weak, good and bad, just and callous. If we try to eliminate emotion from individual and institutional lives, we do not only deny our humanity, but we also ignore so much of what inspires us and makes us better colleagues and better people.

If we want to raise standards, get better, improve the future, equalize opportunity and provide service for others, we therefore cannot and should not set aside our emotions, but we should acknowledge them, understand them, and find ways to articulate and direct them – mitigating their most damaging aspects and making them a resource for the idea of betterment that brings improvement, justice and service together in one common cause.

Emotional change and leadership

Emotions are integrally and intimately associated with change. The Latin origin of emotion is *emovere*: to arouse or stir up. Our emotions are what makes us feel high or low, up or down. They are what leads us to fall in love or to have a 'rush' of excitement. Change, too is about movement – the transformation from one state to another. There is no emotion without change and no change without emotion.

Leadership is also about change. While management involves the efficient organization or coordination of what already exists, leadership changes what exists. Leadership is intended influence. It moves people from one place to another when initially they might have not thought themselves interested in, willing to or capable of doing so. Moses moved his people to the Promised Land, Jack Welch and Michael Rose turned around the failing companies of General Electric and Marks & Spencer. Wangari Maathai mobilized thousands of women to reforest the land across East Africa. All behaved as leaders, not managers. However, Hitler, Stalin and Milosevic were able to move their people too, but not in the way we would admire. In this respect, while leadership, change and emotion all involve movement, the movement is not always in the right direction or necessarily good.

Passion is extreme emotion

Passion can mean 'powerful emotion' directed towards a significant cause, as we have seen in the admirable and execrable instances of the leaders described above. Passion can equally mean 'boundless enthusiasm'. Many supporters of sports teams are passionate, but so are the followers of Osama Bin Laden and Milton Friedman. Passion can also mean martyrdom, such as in the 'Passion of Christ' or of the suicide bombers in the Middle East. Passionate leadership therefore, involves deeply held and intensely felt emotions about causes, principles, ideologies or people. It can be good or bad, useful or destructive, courageous or cowardly. It all depends on the purposes towards which passion is directed and whether leaders are in control of their passions and the people and purposes they serve, or whether their passions are the masters of them.

The point of passionate leadership, then, is not to advocate for more or less, but to understand and acknowledge that leadership is always an emotional practice and sometimes a passionate one and to investigate how leaders can best use and express their emotions and their passion to benefit those they serve, rather than to indulge or subsume the self.

The emotions of educational leadership

If emotions have always been integral to organizational leadership, they have emerged with particular prominence in leadership theory and practice within recent years. There are a number of reasons for this:

■ The movement from a manufacturing to a service and then a knowledge economy means that work with people, communication and symbols is not now confined to marketing and sales departments, or management teams but it is at the heart of everything organizations do (Hochschild, 1983).

■ The growing service economy combined with almost 50 years of women's control over their own fertility, has brought more women into the workplace and then to leadership where some have used their greater emotional awareness and abilities as explicit assets rather than disruptive liabilities (Marshall et al., 2006).

■ Psychological research has kept pace with corporate developments, moving from dominant concerns with perception and cognition, into studies of emotional intelligence (Goleman, 2005; Goleman et al., 2002), learned optimism (Seligman, 2006) and emotional resilience (Viscott, 1996) that are associated with heightened organizational performance.

■ Critics point out that psychological research on emotions has been exploited and expanded by corporations to manipulate customers into making irrational purchases – for instance, by inciting children to use a range of 'nagging' strategies to get their parents to purchase company products (Schor, 2004) – and to extract the final dregs of profitability and surplus value from an already exhausted workforce (Fineman, 2000).

■ Finally, in government and everyday life, Mestrovic (1997) and others (eg. Hartley, 2007) point out that, ironically, it is just at the point when organizations and management have reached their most clinical and technocratically rational by emphasizing targets, performance, prescription, compliance and control, that a compensatory discourse has emerged that highlights and celebrates the emotions. This is evident in consumer goods advertisements that invest cars and cell phones with passion and desire, in executive keynote addresses to lift the workforce and in small spectacles of employee awards that have little bursts of effervescent emotion released within them. Emotions seem to become most prominent in popular leadership theory, just when there is least acknowledgement of or engagement with them in management practice.

Through this unholy alliance of demographic, academic and corporate developments, emotions have now come more explicitly to the fore in leadership and organizational theory. Whereas management texts and titles used to be characterized by words like success, advantage, competition, and excellence; they are now suffused with an emotional language of resilience, vulnerability, confidence, endearment and heart (Kanter, 2004; Kotter and Cohen, 2002; Sheffi, 2005; Sisodia et al., 2007).

These movements have made themselves felt in educational leadership and administration. Though the Human Relations tradition of management and administration has paid tribute to the personal dimensions of leadership for more than half a century (Homans, 1951), Daniel Goleman's (2005) best-selling work on emotional intelligence has really brought the emotional aspect of leadership into centre stage.

Drawing on scholarship in positive psychology, Goleman has argued that in leadership performance, emotional intelligence adds value to cognitive intelligence – turning merely good performers into stars. By being aware of and able to express as well as manage their emotions, by being able to motivate themselves and others around them and by empathizing with diverse groups of employees, clients and leadership teams, emotionally intelligent leaders are said to be more organizationally successful. Some leaders have already developed strong emotional intelligence, Goleman argues, through having experienced nurturing relationships in early childhood and adolescence – but all of us, he claims, can improve our emotional intelligence and effectiveness as adults, through structured programmes of coaching and training.

Goleman et al., (2002), more than anyone, has put emotions into the limelight of leadership. But the way he has done this has come in for considerable criticism. By psychologizing emotions as trainable individual capacities, some say, he has played down or diverted attention from how organizations and their leaders wreak emotional havoc on their employees by bullying them, pitting them against one another or burning them out (Boler, 1999). Captured and seduced by his corporate market, perhaps, Goleman's work also has a tendency, others argue, to concentrate on easily enhanced and rectified emotions like optimism or anxiety, but not on more difficult or complex emotions like envy (that is created by corporate competition) or disgust (the basic emotion of racism) (Fineman, 2000). There is also a tendency for work on emotional intelligence to universalize emotions and to fail to grasp how the way people express and manage their emotions varies across cultures and among different professions like nurses, funeral directors and debt collectors who are all expected to have specific emotional ways of being. The emergent research on the emotions of educational leadership takes up these criticisms and explores leaders' emotional lives less individualistically, prescriptively and simplistically. It pays more attention to the context of emotional interaction and not just to emotional capacities and skills, and it deals with the positive and negative aspects of leaders' emotional lives rather than just those that suggest easy training solutions.

Leaders' emotional lives are often complex, ambivalent and mysterious – invisible to others and sometimes ineffable to leaders themselves. Chris James, Michael Connolly, Gerald Dunning and Tony Elliott (2006) draw on psycho-dynamic training to ask leaders to reflect on how the patterns of their adult leadership interactions with others are often rooted in and replayed from childhood relationships with parents. These include the dangerous tendency to idealize colleagues as wholly good until they let us down when we then demonize them as wholly bad. The impulsive drive to repair the broken schools that remind some leaders of their childhood years in broken homes, or the sublimation of sexual desire and energy in collegial relationships with others are also examples of how we can easily be hijacked by our emotional subconscious (Harris, 2007; Saltzberger-Wittenberg et al., 1983).

Richard Ackerman and Pat Maslin-Ostrowski (2002) ask 'wounded leaders' who are hurt by their disappointments, by the deaths of students or colleagues, or by the bullying and betrayals of superiors, to accept and express rather than deny their vulnerability. In this way, they argue, leaders become more human, more open to being cared for as well as caring, more connected to and therefore even more capable of leading others around them.

Leaders are always engaged in relations of power. They do not therefore just possess or lack the psychological capacities of emotional intelligence, or have greater or lesser mastery over their emotional subconscious. They are also always embroiled in emotional politics. Blase and Blase (2002) document the manifold forms of subtle and blatant emotional bullying that leaders use to silence the teachers who work for them through threats, favouritism, involuntary transfers, gossip, game playing, withheld references, undesirable assignments and accusations of failing to be a team player. Beatty (2002) goes further by arguing that the technocratic emphasis on an emotionally cleansed world of standards, performance and line management amplifies a resounding silence about emotions and about the importance of acknowledging that emotional knowledge is integral to learning, teaching and leadership. Jill Blackmore (1996), meanwhile, describes how women's capacities for caring have been exploited by top-down, technocratic governments as they have turned increasing numbers of women principals into emotional middle-managers of unwanted and imposed educational reforms. These female leaders labour emotionally to motivate their staffs, to implement the unpalatable and impractical policies of government, losing something of themselves and their health in the process.

All educational leadership is emotional leadership, by design or default. Simply to celebrate leaders' emotionality is to ignore its negative and damaging aspects. Only concentrating on training individuals in emotional capacity overlooks the responsibilities of organizations and also governments for the emotional health of leaders (Harris, 2007; PricewaterhouseCoopers LLP, 2007). Accepting that all leadership has an emotional dimension is essential. Understanding how organizations influence leaders' emotionality and to what effect is an essential step forward in helping ensure that passionate leadership becomes positive and purposeful leadership.

Emotional understanding and misunderstanding

I have not directly studied the emotions of leaders. But I have investigated and written about the emotions of teaching – including in relation to teachers and leadership. This work is based on interviews and analysis of critical incidents among 50 Canadian teachers, in relation to positive and negative emotional experiences with colleagues, students, parents and administrators. Two concepts are essential to this work and also in understanding the emotional work of educational leaders: *emotional understanding* and *emotional geographies* (Hargreaves, 1998a, 1998b, 1998c, 1999, 2000, 2001a, 2001b, 2002, 2004, 2005; Hargreaves and Lasky, 2005; Hargreaves and Moore, 1999; Hargreaves and Tucker, 1991).

The concept of *emotional understanding* was invented by sociologist Norman Denzin (1984). Emotional understanding takes us beyond viewing emotions as a set of individual and trainable capacities. Rather, it regards emotions as being embedded in relationships among people and, to some extent, *between* them – rather than solely inside them. Emotional understanding, Denzin says,

> *is an intersubjective process requiring that one person enter into the field of experience of another and experience for herself the same or similar experiences experienced by another. The subjective interpretation of another's emotional experience from one's own standpoint is central to emotional understanding. Shared and shareable emotionality lie at the core of what it means to understand and meaningfully enter into the emotional experiences of another.* (p.137)

Teaching, learning and leading all draw upon emotional understanding as people reach into the past store of their own emotional experiences to interpret and unravel, instantaneously, at-a-glance, the emotional experiences and responses of others. Denzin (1984) describes how emotional understanding can be established through a number of means, including emotional 'infection' (spreading optimistic or pessimistic moods to others); vicarious emotional understanding (where we empathize with people's lives or predicaments through theatre or literature, for example); sharing emotional experience (as when families experience a wedding or bereavement); and by developing long-standing, close relationships with others.

Without close relationships of emotional understanding, educational leaders (indeed anyone) are prone to experience emotional misunderstanding where they 'mistake their feelings for feelings of the other' (Denzin, 1984: 134). Where such close relationships do not exist in schools, teachers can easily misconstrue student exuberance for hostility, or teacher silence for agreement, for example.

Emotional misunderstanding strikes at the foundations of educational leadership. When school leaders forget the challenges of the classroom, or have only fleeting interaction with their staff, they undermine the emotional bonds that tie teachers to their school and its students. Emotional understanding is achieved not just by acts of personal will, sensitivity or virtue. It is not simply a kind of emotional competence or intelligence. Similarly, emotional misunderstanding arises not just because of personal flaws or deficiencies in empathy or other emotional competences. Rather, as Denzin (1984) argues, emotional misunderstanding is a pervasive and chronic feature of everyday interactions where human engagements are not based in this kind of shared experience that fosters close and common understanding. Organizations create these conditions that promote emotional understanding or misunderstanding. This occurs through what I call emotional geographies of interaction.

Emotional geographies

Emotional geographies, as developed from the data we collected from our 50 teachers, and the circumstances that created positive or negative emotion for them, consist of:

> *the spatial and experiential patterns of closeness and/or distance in human interactions and relationships that help create, configure and colour the feelings and emotions we experience about ourselves, our world and each other.* (Hargreaves, 2001b: 1061)

This concept of emotional geographies helps us identify the supports for and threats to the basic emotional bonds and understandings of schooling that arise from forms of distance or closeness in people's interactions or relationships.

My research with teachers identifies five key emotional geographies of teaching: moral, cultural, professional, political, and physical. The rest of this chapter explores the nature and significance of these geographies for educational leaders and leadership. It draws its examples from three research and evaluation projects: my work with Ivor Goodson and Dean Fink of *Change Over Time?* based on almost 300 interviews with teachers and leaders in eight US and Canadian and secondary schools about their experiences of educational change over more than 30 years (Hargreaves and Fink, 2006; Hargreaves and Goodson, 2006); research with Dennis Shirley evaluating leadership behaviour and its effects in a network of 300 underperforming UK secondary schools with the title of *Raising Achievement/Transforming Learning* (RATL) (Hargreaves et al., 2006);

and an evaluation for OECD of the relationship between leadership and school improvement in high-performing Finland (Hargreaves et al., 2007).

Moral geographies

Emotional geographies of distance and closeness are partly embodied in the purposes that people invest in and attach to their professional work. For Lazarus (1991) and his followers in education (Veen and Sleegers, 2006), emotions are entirely about the fulfilment or frustration of people's purposes – though this theory has difficulty dealing with a number of emotions like disgust or surprise. However, there is good evidence that the emotional labour that people undertake when they are working with clients, as they try to be enthusiastic, optimistic, or calm as the job requires, is rewarding when it helps them achieve their purposes, but draining when these purposes are imposed upon them or belong to someone else (Stenross and Kleinman, 1989).

Positive emotion occurs when purposes are clear, achievable, personally meaningful and shared with others. Negative emotion arises when purposes are vague, unrealistic, too numerous to choose from, unwanted or imposed. In our work on emotions of teaching, we found that teachers experience positive emotion when they have a sense of accomplishment with their students, when colleagues agree with their actions, when parents praise rather than criticize them, and when change is self-initiated rather than coming from afar.

Passionate leaders are intense about their purposes. In their classic study of long-lasting companies, for example, Collins and Porras (1994) discovered that such companies had 'a core ideology that transcended pure economics considerations'. In my investigations of the emotions of educational change, I found that many positive changes that teachers described as being self-initiated actually had an outside origin – the schools' leaders had simply been able to convert external reforms into internal initiatives that fit people's purposes. In my work with Dean Fink on *Sustainable Leadership* (2006), we also found that principals succeeded and were satisfied when they acted as guides, helping their staff fit outside reform requirements to the school's learning priorities. But like the principal who sequestered himself in the office to write elaborate responses to government initiatives before circulating them to staff, leaders who tried to shield or over-protect their staffs and did not share or develop purposes with them, turned into unappreciated and disgruntled martyrs.

Purposes, therefore, are emotionally powerful, but they are most positive when they are shared with others rather than shouldered alone, and when policy frameworks give school headteachers genuine opportunity to participate in truly distributed leadership rather than merely delegating tasks to others. Principals in high-performing Finland, for example, feel satisfied with their work because they feel part of a 'society of experts' in their school, who decide policy together. Appointed from their staffs, and working on their behalf, if they should falter or become sick, the staff simply take over the school, seeing that it belongs to all of them, not the principal alone. And the sense of responsibility for a common purpose does not only spread throughout the school but extends across the city and society as Finns, together, feel part of a greater national vision to build a creative, successful and inclusive society.

Finnish principals and schools can concentrate on their purposes, they say, because they are 'not always having to respond to external initiatives like in the "Anglo-Saxon countries"'. In Anglo-Saxon countries, too many educational leaders have been turned into managers – delivering government's political purposes rather than being able to develop or being interested in developing their own. In the UK *Raising Achievement/Transforming Learning* (RATL) project, headteachers found great value in working on clear, practical goals related to improvement, but often felt derailed by the unending interruptions of government initiatives. And in the project studying *Change Over Time?*, one teacher spoke for many when he described the changes he had seen across five different leaders over the years. In the 70s and 80s, he said, the schools' principals,

> *were totally committed to the overall program of the school. Their number one focus was the school. As time went on and principals changed, the principal was less interested in the school and more interested in his own personal growth ... I get to (recent principal) and his number one focus wasn't on [the school]. It was on the next step to be superintendent.*

The moral implications of the emotional geographies of educational leadership are therefore for leaders to be clear about their core purposes, to develop those purposes with others in genuinely distributed rather than merely delegated leadership, and to use their shared purposes to guide the school and students through the political labyrinth of educational change. At the same time, it is important to be alert to the fact that imposing politically expedient policies on schools turns leaders into line-managers and pursuing purposes single-handedly, makes managers into martyrs.

Political geographies

Emotions are not just psychological and personal. They are also political. This is especially true in leadership, which involves exercising power over and with others. Many of the power words for status are the same words for emotion and for space – high/low, up/down, in/out, included/excluded (Shields, 1991). Leadership is therefore not only about trainable emotional intelligence but also about the exercise of emotional politics (Hargreaves, 1998a; Kemper, 1990). Similarities of power create conditions that help support emotional understanding while power disparities and status easily disrupt that understanding – although ironically, in status terms, as Freud understood, it is often the tyranny of minor difference relative to others in salary, status or career progress, that creates the greatest envy and upset (Runciman, 1966; Schwartz, 2004).

People feel emotionally positive when they feel secure, free from threat, in control of their own lives and allowed as well as encouraged to achieve their purposes. Operating within a system that provides high flexibility to schools and resources for them 'to solve their own problems' within the context of an inspirational shared national vision, this is how Finland's principals describe their work.

Negative emotional politics lower people's status through shaming, through creating feelings of insecurity and uncertainty by sanctions and threats, and through overwhelming as well as overruling people's purposes, so they no longer feel in control of their lives. In some cases, leaders are increasingly likely to refuse the opportunity to take on headships, or they retire from them early, because of the conditions of the job that make them politically and publicly vulnerable and subject to sanctions for failing to deliver others' unwanted and often ethically suspect purposes (Pricewater-houseCoopers LLP, 2007). Much of the reason for the generational crisis of leadership succession is attributable to the emotional politics of leadership in a high-stakes era of standardization. Among the Canadian principals involved in our study of *Change Over Time?*, during the age of standardization from the mid 1990s onwards, a high proportion left public education early, making their exits into doctoral study, early retirement, the independent sector, the superintendent's office, or psychiatric care!

But headteachers and principals can be perpetrators of negative emotional politics just as much as they are often the victims of it (Blase and Blase, 2002). This is most evident in the analysis undertaken by Brenda Beatty (2002) of teachers' emotional interactions with their leaders, as part of the *Emotions of Teaching* project. When teachers portrayed positive and negative emotional incidents in interaction with their administrators, the great majority of accounts concentrated on relationships with students, teachers' own careers, and the general emotional climate that leaders set in the school.

Beatty (2002) describes how teachers experience positive emotion, when administrators show respect, care, and professional support for them in these key areas. Recognition through praise, thanks, and commendations as well as being re-hired are evidence of respect. Care and connectedness are displayed through consulting teachers on key ideas, being approachable, knowing about and making allowances for personal and family difficulties, showing that teachers are cared for, trusted and known, and being able to apologize and admit mistakes. Professional support is demonstrated in encouraging teachers to pursue their own professional interests, rather than always having them aligned with the principal's priorities, and in providing back-up and support during difficulties with parents and students.

Conversely, Beatty found, negative emotion and misunderstanding arise when teachers are suppressed and silenced through disrespectful and sometimes public reprimands, interference with their careers, dismissal of their concerns and failure to provide praise or positive feedback. Suspicion or insensitive communication is evidence of lack of care. Finally, absence of professional support and outright betrayal are demonstrated by failure to fulfil promises, unwillingness to provide teachers with support when they experience student problems and the assignment of unsuitable classes for teachers to teach.

These political aspects of emotional geographies suggest a need for greater sensitivity and consideration in leaders' exercise of power. Even the great soccer manager – Arsenal's Arsene Wenger – spends valuable time with his injured players away from the training field, so they do not feel left out (Rivoire, 2007). But more importantly still, as in the case of Finland, these issues suggest a need for more flattening of power differences between governments and schools, leaders and teachers, and schools in relation to each other. Otherwise negative emotional politics will drain all the positive power from our most committed and caring leaders and attract into leadership instead those managers, manipulators and tyrants who are drawn to power only for the benefits it can provide for their own ambitions.

Cultural geographies

Emotions are not the same across all cultures. People experience and express them differently. Secondary emotions especially, like pride, guilt and shame are anthropologically variable (Lupton, 1998). Norbert Elias (1991), for example, points out that Americans prize individual achievement more than the Japanese and therefore experience greater frustration and disappointment when they cannot achieve their purposes. Cultural differences can create distances and barriers to emotional understanding, unless there are deliberate efforts to bring cultures together.

In the *Emotions of Teaching* project, some teachers tended to label lower class or minority parents who questioned their judgement in stigmatized vocabularies of psychological deficiency as 'crazy', 'nuts', 'mad' or 'screamers'. Or they depicted them through polluting verbs of disgust as people who 'grilled' them, 'vented' all over them, or 'blurted' things into their face.

One of the project's team members, Sonia James-Wilson (2001), discovered that when asked what was their ethno-cultural identity and how this affected their emotions, only white, Anglo-Saxon Canadians said they had no particular identity and that their emotionality was therefore not really shaped by it. They made allowances for the emotionality of children from other cultures, they said, but somehow saw their own ethno-cultural identity and emotionality as standard, neutral or superior.

A task of educational leaders is to grasp that their own and their teachers' emotionality is always ethno-culturally particular – needing to be engaged and exchanged with the ethno-culturally variable emotions of parents and students in a quest for greater emotional respect, appreciation and understanding.

Cultures also vary organizationally. Each subject department, and each clique of enthusiastic or reluctant teachers is, in a way, its own emotional country. Emotionally unimaginative managers, like many of the principals in the traditional schools within the *Change Over Time?* study, kept their departments separate, emotionally and intellectually insulated from each other – and delegated tasks to their headteachers. More inspirational leaders brought departments together to share literacy strategies or to build learning communities – enduring initial emotional awkwardness in the quest for greater understanding later on. And in the UK *RATL* project, one of the most turned around schools involved a headteacher who took his most resistant teachers, understood that their disgruntlement was a result of disenchantment with the failure of past reform efforts, and re-engaged them by asking them to reclaim and re-use the lost skills of curriculum development from the 1970s, in order to deliver a motivating programme for the school's most disadvantaged students.

Politics are not the death knell of emotional understanding or improvement. The task of governments and leaders rather, should be to develop *power with* others rather than becoming trapped in chains of power *over* them.

Professional geographies

Professional geographies are distanced by definition. The classical origin of professions emphasizes provision of service to clients in a way that also protects professionals' autonomy through possession of esoteric knowledge, long periods of training and monopolies over service (Etzioni, 1969). Indeed, codes of professional conduct stress the importance of not getting too close to or personally involved with clients.

Yet professions and professionalism are in transition. Internet access distributes medical knowledge widely. There is more competition for and choice over services, and while doctors remain knowledgeable about treatment, more credence is being given to patients' practical knowledge about their own health and bodies (Gawande, 2007). In education too, school data have been made more public, and greater choice has pushed more power the parents' way. At its best, a new professionalism can bring educational leaders closer to their teachers and to parents in more transparent and open relationships.

In our work on the emotions of teaching however, teachers often resented interference from parents and protected their professional autonomy jealously. As one said in response to a parent who questioned her grades, 'I'm the expert. I'm the one with the degrees. She's supposed to be here to help!'

Old constructions of professionalism can likewise encourage school leaders to become estranged from their communities and aloof from their staff. In our *Change Over Time?* study, however, principals of innovative schools who were more open about their professionalism, readily engaged their communities in the design and development of their schools. Equally, disappointing data about achievement or attendance were not withheld from communities but shared openly with them, so they could work on improvement together. Like the Finnish communications company, Nokia, these principals believed that bad news must travel fast (Haikio, 2002; Sheffi, 2005).

New professional geographies can develop rather than diminish emotional understanding between leaders and others if confident and knowledgeable leaders can be open and transparent without feeling too vulnerable, and become more human and personal, without being improper.

Physical geographies

Physical geographies are the organization and distribution of time and space that draw people together or keep them apart, sustain their relationships or truncate them into fleeting interactions. In our emotions of teaching study for example, teachers had negative emotional encounters with parents when face-to-face parents' nights meetings lasted only a few minutes and when communications were mainly confined to phone calls, notes and emails. At these times, it was usually bad news or complaints that initiated interactions.

In our *Change Over Time?* study, some leaders were able to build strong learning communities – in part, by using time and space well to group teachers into teams across disciplines, to create opportunities for shared professional learning and to organize periodic retreats. Visibility and mobility of principals around their schools also enabled difficulties to be anticipated, praise to be distributed and interest to be shown in an easy and effortless manner. However, dissonance and difficulties started to arise when an incoming government reduced resources for preparation time, and overloaded schools with extraneous and unwanted reform requirements – with the result that communities of patient collaboration turned into hurried meetings directed at implementation.

Trends towards accelerated leadership succession that are precipitated by demographic turnover and by political preoccupation with school failure, pose further threats to emotional understanding. Among the Canadian schools in our *Change Over Time?* study, one school had six principals in its first 68 years, then five in a fifth of that time. Another school had just five principals in 28 years, then three in quick succession in the next five. Yet another had four principals in its first 14 years then just as many in the past five. No wonder teachers felt that principals were less and less attached to their schools and more interested in their own careers!

Studies of soccer management show that the greatest long-term success comes from high leadership stability (Bolchover and Brady, 2004). This was also a feature of the ten high-performing primary schools in disadvantaged communities in Wales studied by Chris James et al. (2006). Like many of these Welsh leaders, Finnish leaders too are typically promoted from within their schools where they have become attached to their communities and known by their staffs. This is not an argument for more leaders to stay in their schools in perpetuity – but it does present a case for more, rather than less leadership stability, for smooth strategies of succession, and for greater distribution of leadership so that emotional understanding does not overly depend on the ubiquitous availability in time and space of one woman or one man!

Conclusion

Leadership is always emotional and is sometimes even passionate. Emotional intelligence training can enhance the capacities of individual leaders so their passions are purposeful rather than unruly. Likewise, understanding the importance of emotional geographies helps us grasp what leaders, organizations and policy makers need to do to strengthen the emotional understanding that is at the heart of effective and sustainable improvement, by clarifying and sharing purposes, redistributing power, connecting different cultures, reorganizing time and space, and becoming more professionally transparent. Emotional leaders can be turned into effective leaders who lead through enhanced emotional understanding. Through these means, our educational system might then be guided not by managers who deliver implementation of other people's political demands, but by leaders who inspire purposeful improvement among communities together.

References

Ackerman, R. H., and Maslin-Ostrowski, P. (2002). *The wounded leader: How real leadership emerges in times of crisis*. San Francisco, CA: Jossey-Bass.

Beatty, B. (2002) *Emotion matters in educational leadership*. Unpublished Ph.D. dissertation, University of Toronto, Toronto.

Blackmore, J. (1996) 'Doing "emotional labour" in the education market place: Stories from the field of women in management', *Discourse: Studies in the Cultural Politics of Education, 17*(3): 337–49.

Blase, J. and Blase, J. (2002) *Breaking the Silence: Overcoming the Problem of Principals' Mistreatment of Teachers*. Thousand Oaks, CA: Corwin Press.

Bolchover, D. and Brady, C. (2004) *The 90-Minute Manager: Business lessons from the dugout* (revised ed.). London: Prentice Hall Business.

Boler, M. (1999) *Feeling Power: Emotions and education*. London: Routledge Press.

Collins, J. and Porras, J. (1994) *Built to Last: Successful habits of visionary companies*. New York: Harper Business.

Damasio, A. (1994) *Descartes' Error*. New York: Grosset Putnam.

Darwin, C. (1965) *The Expression of the Emotions in Man and Animals*. Chicago, IL: University of Chicago Press.

Denzin, N. (1984) *On Understanding Emotion*. San Francisco, CA: Jossey-Bass.

Elias, N. (1991) *The Society of Individuals*. Oxford: Basil Blackwell.

Etzioni, A. (1969) *The Semi-Professions and their Organization: Teachers, Nurses, Social Workers*. New York: Free Press.

Fineman, S. (ed.) (2000) *Emotion in Organizations*. London: Sage.

Gawande, A. (2007) *Better: A Surgeon's Notes on Performance*. New York: Metropolitan.

Goleman, D. (2005) *Emotional Intelligence: Why it Can Matter More than IQ* (10th Anniversary edn). New York: Bantam.

Goleman, D., Boyatzis, R. E. and McKee, A. (2002) *Primal leadership: Realizing the power of Emotional Intelligence*. Boston, MA: Harvard Business School Press.

Haikio, M. (2002) *Nokia: The Inside Story*. Helsinki: Edita.

Hargreaves, A., Halász, G. and Pont, B. (2007) *School Leadership for Systemic Improvement in Finland*. Paris: OECD.

Hargreaves, A. and Fink, D. (2006) *Sustainable Leadership*. San Francisco, CA: Jossey-Bass.

Hargreaves, A. and Goodson, I. (2006) 'Educational change over time? The sustainability and nonsustainability of three decades of secondary school change and continuity', *Educational Administration Quarterly*, 42(1): 3–41.

Hargreaves, A., Shirley, D., Evans, M., Johnson, C. and Riseman, D. (2006) *The Long and the Short of Raising Achievement: Final Report of the Evaluation of the 'Raising Achievement, Transforming Learning' Project of the UK Specialist Schools and Academies Trust*. Chestnut Hill, MA: Boston College.

Hargreaves, A. (2005) 'Educational change takes ages: Life, career and generational factors in teachers' emotional responses to educational change', *Teaching and Teacher Education*, 21(2005): 967–83.

Hargreaves, A. and Lasky, S. (2005) 'Parent gap', in J. Sancho, F. Hernandez, A. Hargreaves and I. Goodson (eds) *Social Geographies of Change in Education*. Dordrecht, The Netherlands: Kluwer.

Hargreaves, A. (2004) 'Inclusive and exclusive educational change: Emotional responses of teachers and implications for leadership', *School Leadership and Management*, 24(2): 285–307.

Hargreaves, A. (2002) 'Teaching and betrayal', *Teachers and Teaching: Theory and Practice*, 13(4): 393–407.

Hargreaves, A. (2001a) 'The emotional geographies of teachers' relations with their colleagues'. *International Journal of Educational Research*, 3: 503–27.

Hargreaves, A. (2001b) 'The emotional geographies of teaching', *Teachers'College Record*, 103(6): 1056–80.

Hargreaves, A. (2000) 'Mixed emotions: Teachers' perceptions of their interactions with students', *Teaching and Teacher Education*, 16(8): 811–26.

Hargreaves, A. (1999) 'The psychic rewards (and annoyances) of classroom teaching', in M. Hammersley (ed.), *Researching School Experience: Ethnographic Studies of Teaching and Learning*. (pp. 87–106). Abingdon: Falmer Press.

Hargreaves, A. and Moore, S. (1999) 'The emotions of interpretation and implementation', *Curriculum Perspectives*, 19(3): 1–10.

Hargreaves, A. (1998a) 'The emotional politics of teaching and teacher development: Implications for leadership', *International Journal of Leadership in Education,* 1(4): 315–36.

Hargreaves, A. (1998b) 'The emotional practice of teaching', *Teaching and Teacher Education*, 14(8): 835–54.

Hargreaves, A. (1998c) 'The emotions of teaching and educational change', in A. Hargreaves, A. Lieberman, M. Fullan and D. Hopkins (eds) *The International Handbook of Educational Change*. Dordrecht, The Netherlands: Kluwer.

Hargreaves, A. and Tucker, B. (1991) 'Teaching and guilt: Exploring the emotions of teaching', *Teaching and Teacher Education*, 7(5/6): 491–505.

Harris, B. (2007) *Supporting the Emotional Work of School Leaders*. London: Paul Chapman Publishing.

Hartley, D. (2007) 'The emergence of distributed leadership in education: Why now?', *British Journal of Educational Studies*, 55(2), 202–14.

Hochschild, A. R. (1983) *The Managed Heart: The Commercialization of*

Human Feeling. Berkeley, CA: University of California Press.

Homans, G. C. (1951) *The Human Group*. New Brunswick, NJ: Transaction.

James, C., Connolly, M., Dunning, G. and Elliott, T. (2006) *How Very Effective Primary Schools Work*. London: Sage.

James-Wilson, S. V. (2001) *The Influence of Ethnocultural Identity on Emotions and Teaching*. Paper presented at the Annual Meeting of the American Education Research Association, Seattle, WA.

Kanter, R. M. (2004) *Confidence: How winning streaks and losing streaks begin and end*. New York: Crown Business.

Kemper, T. D. (1990) *Research agendas in the sociology of emotions*. Albany, NY: State University of New York Press.

Kotter, J. P. and Cohen, D. S. (2002) *The Heart of Change: Real-Life Stories of How People Change their Organizations*. Boston, MA: Harvard Business School Press.

Lazarus, R. S. (1991) *Emotion and Adaptation*. New York: Oxford University Press.

PricewaterhouseCoopers LLP. (2007) *Independent Study into School Leadership*. Nottingham: Department for Education and Skills.

Lupton, D. (1998) *The Emotional Self: A Sociocultural Exploration*. London: Sage.

Marshall, C., Wynn, S. and Nowlin, T. (2006) 'Re-papering the room: Leadership theory for women's ways', in *Women as School Executives Monograph Series*, Vol. 6, *Leadership: A Bridge to Ourselves*. Texas: Texas Council of Women School Executives.

Mestrovic, S. G. (1997). *Postemotional Society*. London: Sage.

Rivoire, X. (2007) *Arsène Wenger: The Biography*. London: Aurum.

Runciman, W. G. (1966) *Relative Deprivation and Social Justice: A study of attitudes to social inequality in twentieth-century England*. Berkeley, CA: University of California Press.

Saltzberger-Wittenberg, I., Henry, G. and Osborne, E. (1983) *The emotional experience of learning and teaching*. London: Routledge.

Schor, J. (2004) *Born to Buy: The commercialized child and the new consumer culture*. New York: Scribner.

Schwartz, B. (2004) *The Paradox of Choice: Why more is less* (1st edn). New York: Ecco.

Seligman, M. E. (2006) *Learned optimism: How to change your mind and your life*. New York: Vintage.

Sheffi, Y. (2005) *The Resilient Enterprise: Overcoming vulnerability for com-*

petitive advantage. Cambridge, MA: MIT Press.

Shields, R. (1991) *Places on the margin: Alternative geographies of modernity*. London: Routledge.

Sisodia, R., Wolfe, D. B. and Sheth, J. N. (2007). *Firms of Endearment: How world-class companies profit from passion and purpose*. Upper Saddle River, NJ: Wharton School.

Stenross, B. and Kleinman, S. (1989) 'The highs and lows of emotional labour: Detectives' encounters with criminals and victims', *Journal of Contemporary Ethnography*, 17(4): 435–52.

Veen, K. V. and Sleegers, P. (2006) 'How does it feel? Teachers' emotions in a context of change', *Journal of Curriculum Studies*, 38(1): 85–111.

Viscott, D. (1996) *Emotional Resilience: Simple truths for dealing with the unfinished business of your past*. New York: Harmony.

Building a model of passionate leadership

Chapter 8

Passionate work: towards a natural history of headship

Geoff Southworth

I have often thought that we know more about how animals live in remote jungles than we do about how many humans go about their work. Television documentaries record the patterns of creatures' lives, be it on the Great Plains of Africa, or in the depths of the oceans. Yet, by contrast, we know surprisingly little about the natural history of headteachers.

For teachers, one of the great unanswered questions is 'what do headteachers do all day?' They know their heads and leaders are busy, but even those who work alongside them sometimes find it hard to fathom all the leadership myths, mystiques and mysteries.

Whilst I am being a little flippant here there is also some truth in this opening gambit. This viewpoint explains why I have always been interested in ethnographies of headteachers, be it Wolcott's study (1978) of *The Man in the Principal's Office*, or Hall and her colleagues' study of *Headteachers at Work* (1986). These stimulated my own study into the work of a single headteacher over the course of a school year when I examined what he did and why, and what the staff made of his actions (Southworth, 1995).

Despite the power of these studies to portray headteachers in action, they also, unfortunately, quickly date, particularly in the modern world where change has become ever-present. Moreover, because context is a key feature of leadership, when the contexts in which leaders operate keep changing, then so too must our knowledge of these individuals' work be revised and updated. This is why at the National College for School Leadership (NCSL) in England we

153

have recently been doing two things. First, pulling together what we know about school leadership (NCSL, 2007); and, second, studying leaders in action (NCSL, 2007a).

This second study examined the working lives and practices of 34 headteachers in England. These headteachers were both new and experienced practitioners and from primary, secondary and special schools in a cross section of locations. The study came about, in part, as a result of a series of regional conferences the College hosted at which relentlessness, accountability and complexity of headship emerged as major issues facing the profession. We therefore thought it appropriate to look at leaders' well-being, work–life balance and job satisfaction, as well as using the exercise as an opportunity to update our knowledge of the work practices of headteachers today.

In this chapter I want to draw upon NCSL's research and other recent and relevant studies to outline what headship looks like today. In so doing, I shall concentrate on the patterns that can be seen rather than provide detailed portraits of individuals at work. I also want to link this to the theme of this book – passionate leadership – since this theme touches on leaders' energy, commitment and beliefs.

Headship at the start of the 21st century

Although we know less about headteachers in action than we might wish to know, nevertheless there are many things we are clear about with reference to effective leaders (Leithwood, et al., 2006; NCSL 2007). We know that successful leaders are optimistic, have a vision for the school and a sense of mission in their work. According to Leithwood and his colleagues, successful school leaders:

> ... are open-minded and ready to learn from others. They are also flexible rather than dogmatic in their thinking within a system of core values, persistent (eg. in pursuit of high expectations of staff motivation, commitment, learning and achievement for all), resilient and optimistic. Such traits help to explain why successful leaders facing daunting conditions are often able to push forward when there is little reason to expect progress. (Leithwood, 2006: 14)

It is important to start with the personal qualities of successful leaders because there is plainly something about the dispositions of individuals which matters. In trying to capture what headship in action looks like, it is vital not to overlook the actors themselves. What each brings to the role and stage is as important as the role itself, since their personal traits carry weight in respect of the tone and conduct of actions. Nor is it to suggest that these dispositions are immutable. They can be learned, and indeed are – which is why so much emphasis is placed on leading by example. Leaders are judged by what they do and the way they do these things. And their 'followers' learn what works by watching their leaders. Moreover, lists of those qualities which make a difference serve to remind us that we should always strive to be upbeat, model positivism and strive to be as 'can do' as possible. As someone once said – 'no one wants to follow a cynic'.

Indeed, these qualities tell us something about the emotional intelligence of effective leaders. Those who act in these ways understand that it is important to do so because this is what makes their colleagues feel valued and helps to motivate them, particularly when they are weary and down-hearted. Leadership is strongly concerned with motivating others to come along and join in, as against give up and walk away.

Dispositions and emotional intelligence are then two aspects of effective leadership. Another is a sense of social justice. Many teachers and headteachers have clear sets of values and a strong sense of moral purpose. They are professionally and personally concerned to make a difference to children and the young people in their care. They see schools as places where lives can be changed and pupils' self-esteem raised and life chances enhanced. It is these things which they are often most passionate about.

And for many, the roots of their commitments stem from their own experiences of school and upbringing. For some they want to ensure children have the same opportunities which they benefited from. Others want to make sure that the injustices they felt when at school are never repeated again. The motives of teachers and headteachers are often deeply felt, strongly held and stretch far back into their own childhoods and schooldays.

In other words, personal dispositions and the behaviours we observe in leaders' actions are pointers which help us to understand why leaders do what they do. Research can describe how leaders work and, at the same time, search for what motivates them to behave like that. Looking at leaders' sense of rewards at work and of job satisfaction are two ways of uncovering leaders' values and motives.

The rewards of the job have recently been recorded by the PricewaterhouseCoopers (PwC) team of researchers in their study into school leadership (PricewaterhouseCoopers, 2007). They reported that 'many headteachers and others repeatedly described the unique nature of their role as a "privilege" and a vocation' (p.7).

Their survey of school leaders, across all phases, backed up those comments: nine out of ten headteachers thought that seeing pupils achieve gave them the greatest satisfaction, followed by developing staff and setting the strategic vision. Further details of this survey are shown in Figure 8.1 below:

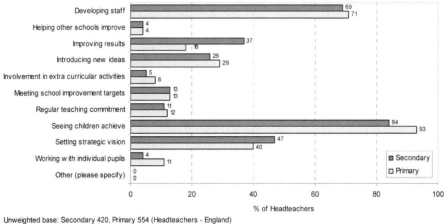

Unweighted base: Secondary 420, Primary 554 (Headteachers - England)
Source: PwC school leadership survey, 2006

Figure 8.1: *Aspects of the headteacher's role that give most satisfaction*
Reprinted with permission of DfES, 2007

PwC also examined the issue of satisfaction from another standpoint. They asked respondents in their survey to list the factors that were influential in keeping them in their post. Highest among the factors were the personal challenge, their contribution to the community, contact with pupils and the success of the school (PwC, 2007: 7).

In research undertaken by Ipsos MORI (2006) into the factors which motivate headteachers, one of the main sources was the non-routine nature of their daily work. It seems headteachers enjoy the range and varied nature of the work. This finding also resonates with earlier work. A qualitative study into headship in primary schools in the 1990s found a similar outlook from the interviewed headteachers. Two explicitly stated gaining job satisfaction from being able to cope with whatever turned up:

> *It's such a changing job. You never know what's going to happen next. There's no predictability to headship ... it is very draining [but also] very rewarding. You do not know what is going to come through the door.*

and

> *I actually like it. It is exciting. There is never a dull moment ... when you are there. You have to be prepared to almost turn somersaults and stand on your head. It is all consuming, all demanding. It is incredibly rewarding.* (Southworth, 1995a: 17)

If citing work from the 1990s in a section focusing on headship in the 21st century seems strange, then it can be explained in terms of role continuities. Whilst headship has undoubtedly changed over time, it has also stayed the same in some respects. Task variety is one of the enduring features of the work and that should not be forgotten if it is a source of satisfaction to some headteachers.

Other motivating factors, according to PwC's fieldwork 'relate to the educational, social and vocational aspects of the role. However, administrative demands and accountability were the main demotivating factors' (PwC, 2007: 7) as Figure 8.2 (over) sets out.

NCSL's research has shown there are three elements of headship which are rated high in terms of reward and job satisfaction:

- developing others
- the nature of the job
- personal relationships.

In terms of developing others, first and foremost this included seeing children progress and succeed:

> *Simply having the children here, seeing them succeed and prepare to be citizens of the 21st century is really rewarding. To see them go home at the end of the day and they've really learnt something that they couldn't do when they arrived is really good.* (NCSL, 2007)

Factors which motivate and demotivate headteachers (Ipsos MORI, 2006)			
Motivating factors	%	Demotivating factors	%
Role is dynamic/not routine	58	Administrative demands	54
Building shared values	54	Inspection/measures of accountability e.g. Ofsted	50
Collegiality/teamwork	46	Low status/negative media image of the profession	41
Job satisfaction/sense of personal achievement	45	Changes in policy	39
Changing social culture	45	External interferences (e.g. LAs, DfES)	39
Maintaining high standards	43	Problems with recruitment/retention	33
Sense of vocation	42	Stress	32
Professional autonomy/implementing own vision	39	Financial responsibilities	20
Passionate belief in the role	38	Less contact with pupils	18
People management (staff)	33	Isolation	15

Ipsos MORI (2006) Base=911

Figure 8.2: *Factors which motivate and demotivate headteachers*
Reprinted with permission of DfES, 2007

Equally, working alongside children, interacting with them at breaks and observing them in lessons were seen as an important and satisfying part of the role. This was expressed by one participant in the following way:

> *Driving to school in the morning – I look forward to coming to work – I don't wake up on a Monday and think 'oh no, I've got to go to work'. I thoroughly enjoy what I do. I enjoy going on the playground in the morning and meeting the children, sitting down together and sharing pupils' achievements, reading their reports, taking a group of kids swimming and seeing them succeed without arm-bands on, succeeding in learning a musical instrument, performing in a production in school.*

Many headteachers also spoke of supporting staff colleagues and seeing them develop too. As to the nature of the job this covered the relatively high levels of autonomy and control they experienced, leading the strategic direction of the school and improving the school. Other factors cited were: receiving positive feedback from parents and others; the variety of the work; and the unpredictability of the job. The latter reinforces the findings of PwC discussed above. Personal relationships included positive dealings with staff and parents, with some headteachers emphasizing the support and comradeship they received from their senior leadership teams, whilst others spoke of being valued by the local community as a source of satisfaction.

The sense of altruism and vocation in all of these findings is very strong and relate to previous comments about vision, motivation and moral purpose. More than anything though it is the sense of making a difference to children's and young persons' lives and learning which comes across. This is the paramount, professional passion of headteachers.

What does a passionate leader look like in action?

The study NCSL conducted into leaders' well-being and work practices, *A Life in the Day of a Headteacher* (NCSL, 2007) involved observing headteachers at work, interviewing them, and asked participating headteachers to complete a journal. Characteristics of the sample of 34 serving heads can be found in the full report on NCSL's website (www.ncsl.org.uk) but, in brief, the sample was split 53 per cent female, 47 per cent male, 21 were primary headteachers, three were headteachers of special schools and ten were secondary headteachers. The schools were located across all nine government office regions of England.

What we found from the study, unsurprisingly, was that headteachers dealt with a lot of things in the course of a working day. In total, 54 different areas of activity were described by participants. Closer inspection of these identified seven broad categories. An eighth category, 'various tasks, unspecified time', was also included for completeness of time – this relates to occasions when individuals were simultaneously undertaking more than one activity, and did not provide an allocation of time for each aspect. Figure 8.3 shows the proportion of time allocated to the eight categories.

What each of the eight categories involved is shown in Figure 8.4, p. 161.

Data from the journals indicated that the participants worked an average of 52.9 hours during the period for which they provided data. In terms of gender, female participants worked longer, with an average 55.4 hours, than male participants who averaged 50.3

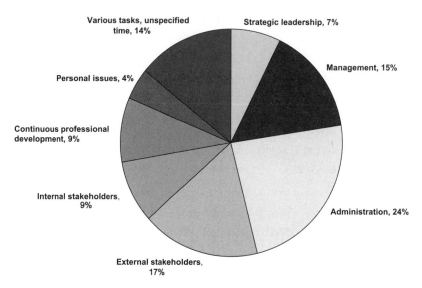

Various tasks, unspecified time, 14%

Strategic leadership, 7%

Management, 15%

Personal issues, 4%

Continuous professional development, 9%

Internal stakeholders, 9%

Administration, 24%

External stakeholders, 17%

Figure 8.3: *Proportion of headteacher time for each broad task group*
Note: Figures do not sum to 100 per cent due to rounding

hours. There were also differences in the hours worked between phases, with special school participants (n=3) working 69.7 hours, compared with 50.1 hours for their colleagues in primary schools (n=21), and 54.3 hours for those in secondary schools (n=10). However, the low number of special school participants in the study means that this finding should to be treated with caution.

There was a pattern observed across the sample of headteachers, which involved long hours during the working week (Monday to Friday), with typically one late evening meeting or event. Coupled with this, participants worked for some period over the weekend. More broadly, workloads were seen as highly demanding by around one-third (32 per cent). Similarly, days themselves were said to be 'fast paced' by around a third of heads (32 per cent). Also, around one-third (29 per cent) saw the workload as 'stressful and draining' and roughly one-sixth (18 per cent) characterized this as 'relentless'.

Given the variety and range of the tasks, at least half of the sample said that there was 'no such thing as a typical day'. This variety, they said, demands considerable flexibility on their part, as they seek to respond to unexpected challenges. One head noted how the activities in his day ranged from 'picking up litter to professional development discussions'. Another noted how this variety resulted in 'a totally fragmented day, with only gaps of sanity'. For some, this

Broad task group	Individual constituent activity
1. Strategic leadership	1. Strategic planning
	2. Leadership meetings
	3. Classroom observations
	4. Self-evaluation form
	5. School improvement plan
2. Management	6. Staff-related issues
	7. Budget and finance management
	8. Behavioural issues
	9. Health and safety issues
	10. Pupils
	11. Premises management including restructuring
	12. Assessment and examination issues
3. Administration	13. General administration
	14. Before- and after-school clubs
	15. Teaching and cover
	16. Travel
	17. Walk around
	18. Playground and lunchtime duties
	19. School trips
	20. Administration appeals and admissions
	21. Assemblies
	22. Phone calls
	23. Emails
	24. Newsletter etc
	25. Letters
	26. Diaries – basic entries
	27. Reading and dealing with post
	28. Special educational needs
	29. References
4. External stakeholders	30. Local authority
	31. Network and other schools
	32. Governors
	33. External – miscellaneous
	34. External assessors
	35. Parents
	36. Community
	37. Social workers
	38. Visitors
5. Internal stakeholders	39. Staff meetings and briefings
	40. Personal assistants and administration staff
	41. Caretaker and site management
6. Continuous professional development	42. Courses and conferences
	43. Headteacher's own development
	44. Reading and personal reflection
	45. Developing other staff, mentoring and coaching
	46. For externals
7. Personal issues	47. Personal time – breaks and lunch
	48. Doctor and dentist appointments
	49. Family
	50. Funeral
	51. Dealing with bad news
	52. Unspecified
	53. Travel
	54. Sport
8. Various tasks, unspecified time	

Figure 8.4: *Summary of broad task groups and individual activities for headteachers*

was seen as one of the main attractions of the job: 'Gruelling week, next week does not promise [that] much [will be] different. Despite this I wouldn't do anything else!' For others, however, it could be a source of frustration.

For almost two thirds such multi-tasking was seen as the norm as they responded quickly to the unexpected demands of the day and sought to address the concerns of staff and students alike. In some instances (15 per cent), these demands were seen as critical and had the potential to dominate the day, blowing other priorities and schedules off track and requiring immediate attention. Such critical instances often centred on the health and safety of students and staff. Examples observed in the study included problems with student behaviour (eg. the exclusion of a student with a knife), staffing issues (eg. sickness and long-term absences relating to complaints and formal procedures) and issues relating to parents (eg. complaints relating to bullying).

A major aspect of the headteachers' work involved responding to the needs of others in their schools. This took a number of different forms and related, in part, to the traditional concept of headship held by children, staff and the wider community. For instance, some participants (9 per cent) had unscheduled meetings with students sent to them for things such as completing a good piece of work. Similarly, parents attending the school were often likely to ask for the headteacher, even though discussions with the classroom teacher may have been as, or even more, worthwhile. In this instance, it was the symbolism of the headteacher role that was critical.

Many of the dealings with staff were light, friendly and undertaken on an ad hoc, face-to-face basis as issues arose. They generally drew considerable support from others in their schools. For example, participants (38 per cent) showed a high level of interdependency with their administrative staff. Indeed, support staff often acted as an important filter, reducing the pressures on the headteacher by dealing with visitors, parents and administrative demands.

Delegation of activities to other staff in their school further reduced the demands of the job for some participants. These practices served to reduce workload to a more manageable level and allowed the headteachers to focus on areas of greater priority. As one headteacher noted:

You'd be crazy not to delegate. And I think that's where a lot of my colleagues are getting bogged down in that admin and data handling work – instead of being out with the children and the team where it matters.

Management and leadership

A considerable amount of the headteacher's days could be seen as dealing with the managerial aspects of the job, eg. handling paperwork (18 per cent) and the development of systems to support the completion of tasks (12 per cent). Many headteachers also stressed the importance of visibility (having a high profile within the school) both for students and staff alike. This was evidenced by practices such as their early arrival at school and their walkabouts during break time and at the start and the end of the day. These strategies were important as they provided opportunities for informal discussion with staff, parents and children plus opportunities to model desired behaviour within the school.

Other issues

'Other issues' cover a range of different things. However, the emotional nature of the job is most noteworthy. Many participants (29 per cent) demonstrated a considerable personal commitment to their work. This high-level investment meant that headship was often something of an emotional roller coaster, with marked highs and lows. Children were invariably core to these contrasting views, with considerable satisfaction coming from seeing them achieve and develop and from simply being in their company (14 per cent). More broadly for some headteachers (18 per cent) the role brought enormous satisfaction, despite its challenges, a sentiment captured by one headteacher who said:

It is the best job in the world and I wouldn't change it.

The PwC survey which was conducted at the same time as NCSL's enquiry shows a broadly similar picture. For example, it shows the tasks headteachers report as taking up most of their time. Whilst the categories do not match exactly those used in the NCSL analysis, there is sufficient consistency for comparisons to be drawn as Figure 8.5 shows.

However, rather than continue to delve into the detail of these studies I want, instead, to offer some generalized observations from this work. There are, it seems to me, some clear patterns here. Moreover, as suggested above, these patterns provide some clues as to why headteachers work like this and what motivates them.

The work is both demanding and time consuming. Headteachers work long hours in term time, and deal with a range of tasks. Multi-tasking is a feature of the work and since much of the work involves talking and listening, a great deal of the role resides within the heads' heads! A lot rests upon being able to keep many things in one's mind. Moreover, headteachers need to process the many pieces of information they have, integrate the key elements and create a coherent perspective (Martin, 2007). The work is a constant process of meaning-making. Heads, like executives and leaders in

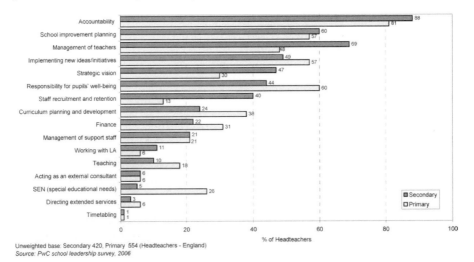

Unweighted base: Secondary 420, Primary 554 (Headteachers - England)
Source: PwC school leadership survey, 2006

Figure 8.5: *Tasks taking up most of headteachers' time*
Reprinted with permission of DfES, 2007

many other jobs, are continually developing interpretations, constructing knowledge and making judgements. Headship is an active process of mind and many seem to enjoy this. It is mentally active work, absorbing and mind-filling, which in turn suggests we might need to look more closely at how effective leaders think, as others have been doing in the commercial sector (Martin, 2007).

School leadership is also emotional labour. Plainly headteachers care for others – first and foremost the children and young people they are responsible for, but also staff and the communities they serve. Much is made today about the emotional intelligence of successful leaders, but perhaps too little is made about the emotional toll of the work. Headteachers, like teachers and others in schools, care deeply about the pupils and are often involved with individual cases of hardship, deprivation and abuse. These cases whilst dealt with professionally also carry an emotional tax, creating concerns, disquiet and worries when too little appears to be happening to help young people and their families. These are proper responses, but they sometimes cause headteachers to have feelings of guilt too: guilt in not having done enough themselves, or soon enough. There is a developing literature on the emotions of teaching (Fox-Wilson, 2003; Sutton and Wheatley, 2004; Hargreaves, 2007), but possibly too little, as yet, on the emotions of school leadership (see Crawford, 2007). Those who are passionate about their work are likely to experience strong emotions – both positive and negative. It seems from the great majority of the work referenced here that these emotions are positive, but for some there may be bleaker moments when negative emotions surface.

The tasks headteachers do, when added together, might also be characterized as 'greedy work' (Gronn, 2003). According to Gronn, such work makes heavy claims on those who do it:

> Greedy work is such that it demands one to be constantly and 'fully there' (Kahn, 1992): always attentive, alert, absorbed in and utterly committed to the particular task as a totally functioning, fully available, non-stop cognitive and emotional presence in the workplace. (Gronn, 2003: 149)

Furthermore, headteaching and teaching are jobs where it is difficult, if not impossible, to ever believe the work is completed. There is a kind of never-endingess to the work, there is always more to do, or more one might have done – both sources of guilt on occasions. This is why school holidays are important because whilst the work may not be finished, it is now suspended for a while and teachers and headteachers can enjoy some 'time out'.

Having studied headteachers in action myself, and listened to many hundreds over the years talk about their work, it seems to me that their work is characterized by brevity, variety and fragmentation, a classification which I believe originates from Mintzberg's (1973) now classic study of managerial work. That variety is one feature has already been established. Brevity relates to the fact that headteachers are often interrupted – telephones, emails, staff, students all homing in on them throughout the day, unless special precautions are taken. Fragmentation covers the fact that headteachers are often switching from one topic to another – so one minute the work is about teaching or curriculum, next it can be financial, equipment, child protection, prospective parents and so on (and on and on).

Yet there is also a 'flow' to the work (Gronn, 1999). As the work moves along over time and patterns form and new tasks evolve and interrelate, then from the incidents, interactions and exchanges leadership itself emerges. If leadership is taken as a form of social influence, then all this work is not stopping headteachers from leading, rather each action is itself a particle of leadership. Each issue is a vehicle for leadership to be exercized. The work flow is significant not because it is preventing heads from leading, but because it is within this flow that leadership is performed.

None of this should overlook the fact that headteachers work long hours and carry heavy workloads. What the NCSL study showed was that it is important for headteachers and other senior leaders to have what occupational psychologists call 'coping strategies'. Coping strategies are the ways individuals find of relieving pressure, giving themselves a break from their work and achieving a balance in their work and lives, suited to their temperaments and needs. In the NCSL study (2007) the coping strategies used by headteachers fell into roughly four categories:

- health and hobbies
- family, friends and personal support
- strategies for managing work
- personal philosophy.

Here it is most relevant to dwell on the last of these. Personal philosophies that enabled headteachers to maintain a sense of work–life balance were important to half the headteachers studied.

A strong mental attitude and training oneself not to succumb to stress were fundamental, said one. Another was strong beliefs. The idea of a moral purpose and personal values was also important for many since this drove them and sustained them. And just under half mentioned having a positive outlook and a sense of humour.

In some ways the importance of personal philosophy touches on the last point to make in this section. Given the demanding nature of the role, it is legitimate to ask, what makes people do this and, equally importantly, keep on doing this for many years? The answer seems to be because they are passionate about what they are striving to accomplish. The work is very important to them, as well as to all those they are trying to serve. Their passion is their work, what they do and how they do it, since effective headteachers know that the medium of leadership has to be the message. As noted above, effective leaders know that it is through the flow of their work that they influence people and make professional allies and supporters. Expressed another way, headteachers' passion for their work stems from personal and professional philosophies which the work sustains and, at the same time, is a vehicle for transacting. Hence for such headteachers their work is a vocation and vocation is another word for life work. The natural history of headship as sketched out here suggests that for those with a passion to lead it is because this is their life work.

Developing passionate leadership for the 21st century

A number of studies, from West-Burnham's notion of 'reservoirs of hope' (2002), and Flintham's study of this concept in practice (Fintham, 2003), to Fullan's work (2003) on moral purpose, show that a leader's values and passion are the fuels which sustain them. This chapter has also argued that it is the leader's higher goals and values which sustain them through the long days and weeks of work. What the portrait sketched out in the previous sections shows is both further evidence of the vital place values have and how vision, values and passion provide an anchor to their work whilst in the midst of turbulent days and times. Explicitly knowing what one's values and vision are provides not only a sense of knowing *where* one is going, but also clarity about *why* that is important.

Values critically, provide meaning to one's actions. They make the difference between, on the one hand, dealing with myriad events and incidents in a noisy, chaotic and seemingly cluttered context and, on the other, being able to bring a sense of coherence to everything one does. An individual's professional passions transform those who would otherwise experience executive 'busyness', into those who see every action as contributing to a greater purpose. Passion changes the way we look at our practice. It gives point, purpose and reason, which is why Fullan's work is so important in this respect because he talks about moral *purpose*.

None of this is to suggest that the way headteachers work today, and the environments they work in should continue as they are. We need to be thinking about how headteachers can be enabled to be even more effective today and tomorrow. Therefore, what I wish to turn to now is how we might possibly improve leadership. There are six aspects to highlight here:

1. Improve leadership preparation and development
2. Improve support for school leaders
3. Accentuate the positive
4. Move away from heroic headship
5. Examine values and visions
6. Encourage leaders to share their values.

Within the limitations of this chapter I will briefly say something about each.

First, it is clear, despite the efforts of the National College, universities, local authorities and many private agencies and consultants, leadership development and headship preparation need to continue to grow and improve. This is why NCSL has invested so much effort into redeveloping the National Professional Qualification for Headship (NPQH). Furthermore, we need to recognize that classroom teaching by itself is not very good preparation for becoming an effective school leader, as Fullan states (2003: 17): 'teachers, as future leaders, obtain only a small slice of what it means to be a headteacher and this 'narrowness of experience is all the more constrained when the teacher's experience is limited to one or two schools'.

We all have to provide prospective leaders with greater knowledge of effective leaders at work, in a range of school contexts and settings. Which is why interest in internships, residencies, placements and assignment-based learning in other schools should increase. We have to provide wider frames of reference for future school leaders and much of this has to be done in schools, alongside the most effective leaders who can coach and transfer their leadership skills and knowledge to others.

Second, improving support for leaders is increasingly important. Headteachers as a group tend to put others first and themselves last when it comes to extra support and resources. Yet there is a convincing case to be made for them now needing to have their fair share of the resources if they are to continue to meet the challenges and changes already under way in society, the communities their schools serve and within their schools. From those schools which employ a school business manager (SBM), who manages the finances and other administrative affairs, we can see that there are many benefits – in terms of efficiencies, savings, income generation and value for money. Where some schools have upgraded and developed more advanced roles for their SBMs, so that they also take on human resource, site and facility management, and join the school's leadership team, there are even greater benefits. It frees the headteacher from these matters on a day-to-day basis, creates time for the headteacher and leadership team to focus on making a difference to children's lives and learning and enables more time for strategic leadership of the school.

Of course, not every school, particularly in the primary sector can afford such a post; but there are many opportunities for groups of schools to jointly fund and work together in federations, or networks to share such a post. In addition to the advantages already mentioned, another important one is bringing into the leadership team new skills and improving the mix of talents to serve 21st century schools, instead of trying to run them on 20th century assumptions and models.

Third, accentuating the positive aspects of leadership and management must become the norm. Passionate leaders are, as noted at the outset, positive, optimistic people. Such outlooks need to be sustained and points one and two go some way towards that. Leaders also need to be refuelled, through opportunities for advanced study, visits, and working beyond their own schools. But support alone will not change hearts and minds. Neither of the first two points will happen if we do not challenge those who see the system as the major fault. Fullan, drawing on Sarason's (1982) study, argued that the tendency of principals and headteachers 'to anticipate trouble from the system is one of the most frequently and major obstacles to trying new procedures' (Fullan, 2003: 18). Fullan then goes on to elaborate by citing 'if-only' thinking as another barrier. It is not that this line of thinking is illegitimate, but that those who use it:

> ... *assume the system must get its act together before people can do their jobs. This is not a very good starting point for practicing principals because it stops them in their tracks.*

Headteachers must work at breaking the bonds of dependency, otherwise they could effectively lose, or surrender their moral compasses. That is why tackling such outlooks is important. It is not that there isn't some truth in the viewpoint, it is the damage such a perspective does to those individuals who subscribe to it. Just as cynical and negative teachers with low expectations blight children's learning, so too can headteachers who see themselves as powerless to make changes because they are dependent on others improving their circumstances lose their agency and drive to make as big a difference as they can. If we allow leaders to become prisoners of such a perspective we are complicit in allowing them to relinquish their responsibilities. In a school system such as England has, which is one of the most devolved systems in the world, we need all headteachers and leaders to believe, along with their staff and colleagues that they can and do make a huge difference. Children and young people respond and deserve to be led by those who have the drive, verve, *élan*, panache, spirit and enthusiasm for the work and the challenges. However these dispositions are enacted – and they can be exercised by extrovert, larger than life characters, as well as quieter, calm and listening leaders – they are necessary because they help to keep alive the passion and the flame for children's achievements and futures.

Fourth, for a number of reasons we need to move away from heroic models of leadership. Of course, there is a place for some heroism. It is evident in failing or struggling schools, which need to be turned around and quickly, that strong and direct leadership is usually necessary for a time. But we also know that heroic leadership is not sustainable over the long term. Moreover, too many people will be 'turned off', or burnt out if the hero model of leadership prevails (HayGroup, 2007). Heroic models infer that leaders are:

> *Authoritative in every situation, knowledgeable in every field, accountable for every action, polished, perfect and relentlessly enthusiastic. This model is deeply rooted in our culture and many job holders conspire to perpetuate it – gaining secret short term satisfaction from sacrifice, troubleshooting, being in demand and even martyrdom.* (HayGroup, 2007: 15)

Essentially this point is about balance. Moral purpose doesn't mean being saintly. Leading with passion must be feasible for all headteachers committed to wanting to make a difference (Fullan, 2003: 30). Passionate and visionary leaders can become zealots, or missionaries; and sometimes missionaries become martyrs! We need to be aware of the dangers of excessive evangelism and have a sense of proportion about one's passions.

Which is why the fifth point is not so much the last, as the first and foremost one. Leaders must critically examine their values and vision. When Hallinger and Heck (2002) asked the question 'what do you call people with visions?' they responded by listing the following possibilities: a) insane, b) religious fanatics, c) poets, d) mystics, e) leaders (p. 9). No doubt we could add some others. The foundation of vision is moral or spiritual in nature and it draws on its power as a wellspring of personal motivation that can act as a catalyst to action for oneself and, potentially, for others (Hallinger and Heck, 2002: 10). My point is that one person's passion and mission may be someone else's puzzle, or predicament. Anyone in a responsible position in a democratic society must be willing to put their ideas to the test and be ready and able to explain and defend their position. Leadership is a social activity and professional leadership should be based on sound professional knowledge and judgements, not shallow opinions, or with scant regard to evidence, or experience. The underpinning values should be surfaced, interrogated and challenged, from time to time, otherwise they become habitual or remain untested. Critical review has to be part and parcel of being a leader. Just as the unexamined life is not worth living, so too is unexamined leadership not worth following – even if they are the most passionate and persuasive of persons – or perhaps because they are!

Sixth, organizations can help aspiring leaders to work well in the realm of values. Headteachers themselves should encourage middle and senior leaders alike to explore their own values and to articulate them in non-dogmatic ways and to express them in their actions (Bennis and Thomas, 2007: xiv). Some leaders avoid articulating what they stand for because of the risk of value conflicts. In fact, values are always present – implicitly if not explicitly, and visible in our actions and words. Therefore, as Bennis and Thomas wisely argue:

> When an organisation's values are clear, participants' perceptions tend to be more accurate and decision-making tends to be simpler and faster. Organisations with clear, shared values are often able to outperform their peers. And values are less likely to be divisive when everyone remembers that tolerance is a key value in a diverse work-place.

Finally

Looking at what leaders do and how they behave is important because it enables us to describe their actions, workloads and work flows. But these are also the surface manifestations of deeper motivations: what lies beneath behaviour, what governs and regulates personal actions is key to understanding leadership.

Underneath all the high energy and activity which characterizes school leaders at work, lies a set of values which constructs their visions and generates their passions. These values sustain them, give them a compass to progress by and provide meaning to their daily and seemingly disparate actions.

A headteacher's values and vision are also the source of their motivation and their starting points for establishing an organizational mission. Organizational mission exists when the personal visions of a critical mass of people cohere in a common sense of purpose within a community. It is part of leadership to engage colleagues and stakeholders in such ways that create a compelling mission to which they all subscribe, are committed to putting into practice and work towards accomplishing. Bringing people together in such a way is often difficult and requires headteachers to be, on occasions, courageous. There was little mention among those headteachers the NCSL studied about courage, but that may well be what they really meant when they talked about determination. It is also another aspect of emotional labour. Among all the personal characteristics which can be listed for effective leadership, such as: strength of character, humility, humour, optimism and passion is emotional resilience. That, though, is something for another study perhaps?

Acknowledgements

Thanks are due to Michael Bristow, Jill Ireson and Katy Emmerson, all members of the Research and Policy team at NCSL for their help in preparing the data and text summaries for this article.

References

Bennis W. and Thomas, R.J. (2007) *Leading for a Lifetime*, Boston, MA: Harvard Business School.

Crawford, M. (2007) 'Rationality and emotion in primary school leadership: an exploration of key themes', *Educational Review*, 59(1): 87–98.

DfES (2007) *Independent Study into School Leadership*. London: DfES.

Flintham, A. (2003) *Reservoirs of Hope: Spiritual and Moral Leadership in Headteachers*. Nottingham: NCSL Practitioner Enquiry Report.

Fullan, M. (2003) *The Moral Imperative of School Leadership*. London: Sage Publications.

Fox-Wilson, D. (2003) *Supporting Teachers, Supporting Pupils: The Emotions of Teaching and Learning*. London: Routledge.

Gronn, P. (1999) *The Making of Educational Leaders*. London: Cassell.

Gronn, P. (2003) *The New Work of Educational Leaders: Changing Leadership Practice in an Era of School Reform*. London: Paul Chapman Publishing.

Hall, V., Mackay, H. and Morgan, C. (1986) *Headteachers at Work*. Buckingham: Open University Press.

Hallinger, P. and Heck, R. (2002) 'What Do You Call People With

Visions? The Role of Vision, Mission and Goals in School Leadership and Improvement', Leithwood, K. and Hallinger, P. (eds), *Second International Handbook of Educational Leadership and Administration*. London: Kluwer, pp. 9–40.

Hargreaves, A. (2007) *The Emotions of Teaching*. San Francisco, CA: Jossey-Bass.

HayGroup (2007) *Rush to the Top: Accelerating the Development of Leaders in Schools*. London: HayGroup.

Ipsos MORI (2006) Follow-Up Research into the State of School Leadership in England. J. Stevens, J. Brown and J. Smith, London: DfES.

Leithwood, K., Day, C., Sammons, P., Harris, A. and Hopkins, D. (2006) *Seven Strong Claims About Successful School Leadership*. Nottingham: NCSL and DfES.

Martin, R. (2007) 'How Successful Leaders Think', *Harvard Business Review*, 85(6): 60–7.

Mintzberg, H. (1973) *The Nature of Managerial Work*. New York: Harper and Row.

NCSL (2007) *What we Know about School Leadership*. Nottingham: NCSL.

NCSL (2007a) *A Life in the Day of a Headteacher: A Study of Practice and Well-Being*. Nottingham: NCSL.

PricewaterhouseCoopers, (2007) *Independent Study into School Leadership*. London: DfES.

Sarason, K. (1982) *The Culture of the School and the Problem of Change* (2nd edn), Boston: Allyn & Bacon.

Southworth, G. (1995) *Looking into Primary Headship: A Research Based Interpretation*. London: Falmer Press.

Southworth, G. (1995a) *Talking Heads: Voices of Experience; an Investigation into Primary Headship in the 1990s*. Cambridge: University of Cambridge Institute of Education.

Sutton, R.E. and Wheatley, R.E. (2004) 'Teachers' emotions and teaching: A review of the literature and directions for future research', *Educational Psychology Review*, 15(4): 327–58.

West-Burnham, J. (2002) *Leadership and Spirituality*. Nottingham: NCSL Leading Edge Seminar Thinkpiece.

Wolcott, H. (1978) *The Man in the Principal's Office: An Ethnography*. Prospect Heights, IL: Waveland Press.

Chapter 9

Enchanted leadership

Brian J. Caldwell

It is rare nowadays to hear that leadership in schools is enchanting. It is even rarer to read a report of research on the theme. A *Google* search yields just one primary reference. Regrettably, it is more common to read about disenchanted leadership. However, there is an aspect of enchantment that has largely escaped attention and it was revealed in a deeper reflection on what it takes to constructively channel passion to the cause of education and on leaders whose words and actions can be fairly described as 'enchanting'. It is possible for passion and enchantment to enter the mainstream of research, theory, policy and practice in leadership, and it is the purpose of this chapter to make a contribution. We certainly need new and uplifting language to enrich the field.

Research on enchanted leadership

The primary reference is *Enchanted Headteachers: Sustainability in Primary School Headship* (Woods, 2002). Ronnie Woods served as a Research Associate at the National College for School Leadership (NCSL) while in post as headteacher of Cleadon Village Junior School, South Tyneside (UK). He set the context in these terms:

> *There are some studies that examine how a headteacher's career develops. Many of them see an inevitable decline; a descent into disenchantment and withdrawal. However there are suggestions that*

this is not necessarily so; there is a view that long-serving head-teachers can be renewed and revitalised by new waves of energy; that there is a route to sustainability and enchantment. (p. 3)

Woods cited research on the careers of secondary headteachers by Day and Bakioglu (1996) that identified four phases: initiation, development, autonomy and disenchantment. Woods sought to challenge the apparent inevitability of this sequence by exploring 'what some of the revitalising waves of new energy might look like' (Woods, 2002: 4). He employed three criteria for enchantment: length of service, effectiveness, and sustained enthusiasm and commitment. He identified the following characteristics of enchanted headteachers based on interviews with those who satisfied the criteria:

- Pride, a selfless pride, a generosity of spirit, a pride in their people and their achievements.
- Closeness to the children and an acute awareness of their needs and where they come from. A belief that their school is making a huge difference to children's lives.
- Passionate commitment to teaching and learning; to the quality of provision, to maintaining high standards, to the development of fully rounded individuals, well prepared for the next stage of their lives. They know what is going on, and everyone knows that they know.
- Respect for, and sensitivity to, the needs of others, placing a high value upon quality of relationships throughout the school com- munity. This respect and sensitivity is modelled strongly in all they say and do. A builder of teams, a developer of people.
- An optimistic view of change as challenge. Not a blind acceptance of change but a view that the school must keep moving forward, can always improve further. Imposed change is to be taken, adapted and made to work in their schools.
- Good at listening, encouraging the contribution of others, accept- ing of constructive criticism and able to admit mistakes. And in doing so to be self-reflective.
- View themselves as nothing special. Acutely conscious that much of what they do and how they do it is context sensitive. (Woods, 2002: 14–15)

There is consistency between the characteristics of enchanted leaders reported by Woods, the elements of Level 5 leadership identified by Collins (2001), and the attributes of exhilarated leaders (Caldwell, 2006). In *Good to Great* Collins drew on research in enterprises that went from being merely 'good' to recognizably 'great', and concluded that there was a hierarchy of leadership capacity, with Level 5 at the top calling for an 'executive leader' who 'builds enduring greatness through a paradoxical blend of personal humility and professional will' (Collins, 2001: 20). Many of the characteristics of such leaders resonate with those of the 'enchanted leader' in Woods's study. For example, the 'executive leader' demonstrates 'an unwavering resolve to do whatever must be done to produce the best long-term results, no matter how difficult' (professional will) and acts 'with quiet, calm determination; relies principally on inspired standards, not inspiring charisma to motivate' (personal humility) (Collins, 2001: 36).

In 2005 the author conducted five workshops on the theme of 'exhilarating leadership'. The purpose was to study the circumstances under which some headteachers seemed to be exhilarated when they were leading schools that had undergone a transformation, often under the most challenging of circumstances. The workshops were conducted in two states of Australia (Victoria and Queensland). Most of the 185 participants were headteachers (principals). They came from a representative cross-section of schools, with most from government or state schools, and the others from non-government (private) subsidised schools, either Catholic systemic schools or independent schools. They came from a variety of socio-economic settings. There was a balance of male and female participants.

Three questions were posed: What aspects of your work as leader are exhilarating? What aspects of your work as leader are boring, depressing, discouraging or dispiriting? What actions by you or others would make your work as leader more exhilarating and less boring, depressing, discouraging or dispiriting? Findings for each question are reported in *Re-imagining Educational Leadership* (Caldwell, 2006). Of particular interest for our current purposes are the responses to the first question.

Participants generated 509 responses to the question, 'What

aspects of your work as leader are exhilarating?' There were some striking features in the pattern of responses. Each of the three top-ranking themes attracted at least 20 per cent of responses, together totalling 67 per cent. Each is concerned with good outcomes. Top ranking (26 per cent) is exhilaration associated with success in a particular project, challenge, problem or grant; second ranking (21 per cent) for good working relationships with and among staff; the third for experiencing and celebrating the accomplishments of students (20 per cent). The dominant pattern is therefore associated with the core purpose of schooling that can be summarized as 'success in tasks related to learning and the support of learning, characterized by fine working relationships with staff, and enjoyment that accompanies good outcomes for students'.

Participants gave a similar number of responses to the second question about experiences they found boring, depressing, discouraging or dispiriting. The point is that they, like the headteachers interviewed by Woods, were able to override the negative to experience exhilaration (enchantment).

Passion and enchantment

What is the essence of enchantment or exhilaration? Is there a place for passion so that passionate leaders can also be enchanted leaders? Can the experience of headteachers also be the experience of system leaders or national leaders including ministers or prime ministers? The answer to the first question can be discerned in the research reported above. An important common element is that enchantment or exhilaration is the result of an interaction between the leader and those with whom he or she works.

Formal definitions can assist. The relevant definition of 'enchant' in the *Merriam-Webster Online Dictionary* is, 'to attract and move deeply' or 'to rouse to ecstatic admiration'. The listed synonyms (attract, allure, charm, captivate, fascinate, enchant) have the common meaning, 'to draw another by exerting a powerful influence'. In teasing out these synonyms, the dictionary suggests that enchant is 'perhaps the strongest of these terms in stressing the appeal of the agent and the degree of delight evoked in the subject'. This adds to our understanding of enchantment, because it is not only the interaction between the leader and others but it is also the response of these others such that the degree of enchantment is dependent on the 'degree of delight'.

An important distinction

It is necessary at this point to distinguish between 'enchanted leadership' and 'enchanting leadership'. The former refers to the emotional response of the leader. The latter may refer to the emotional response of the leader but it also encompasses the emotional response of others to the actions of the leader. The broader concept is adopted in the pages that follow.

Let us turn to the second and third questions posed above. Is there a place for passion? Can enchanting leadership refer also to leaders at the system and national levels? Or even a fourth question: can we construct a theory of passionate leadership that is also enchanting leadership? Our starting point in exploring these questions is the vision of a prime minister who declares a passion for education.

Passion and vision in education

It is remarkable how many national leaders or aspiring national leaders declare a passion for education or in intention to be 'the education president' or 'the education prime minister'. UK Prime Minister Gordon Brown is a case in point. He set out his vision for education in a speech at the University of Greenwich in November 2007 (Brown, 2007). He declared that 'education is my passion' and offered the following explanation:

> *I make no apology for saying that education is the best economic policy. And I make no apology for wanting every child to be able to read, write and add up. But education has always been about more than exams, more than the basics, vital as they are. To educate is to form character, to shape values, and to liberate the imagination. It is to pass human wisdom, knowledge and ingenuity from one generation to the next. It is a duty and a calling. As Plutarch said, the mind is*

not a vessel to be filled but a fire to be kindled. And that is why we have such high ambitions. Not just because education is a matter of national prosperity, although it is certainly that. It is because education is the greatest liberator mankind has ever known, the greatest force for social progress. And that is why it is my passion.

Brown recalled his good fortune in attending a school 'that aimed high [and] that had an ethos of striving, hard work and achievement. And that is what I want for every child in this country. [Hence] Education is my passion'.

These are noble statements about the purposes of education but are they enough to explain why education is 'my passion'? Can Brown be described as demonstrating 'passionate leadership'? It is one thing to make the declaration, even to deliver it passionately, but it is another thing for it to be believable or for it to be a source of energy that brings vision to realization. The vision for Brown was that 'I want to see a Britain where every child can go to a world class school, supported by high aspirations, surrounded by excellent opportunities ... A Britain where effort is rewarded, ambition fulfilled, potential realized' (Brown, 2007).

The relevant definition of 'passionate' in the *Merriam-Webster Online Dictionary* is 'having or expressing great depth of feeling', which is the same meaning ascribed to 'fervent', and it is the list of synonyms for each word that charges them with emotion. They include ardent, blazing, burning, fiery, flaming, glowing, hot-blooded, red-hot, and vehement. Antonyms or near antonyms include cold, cool, detached, dispassionate, dry, impersonal, impassive, objective, reserved, undemonstrative and unemotional.

Of particular interest is whether Brown was demonstrating not only passionate leadership but also enchanting leadership. Recall the essence of enchantment: to enchant is to 'rouse to ecstatic admiration'. Whether or not a person's leadership can be described as enchanting depends on the response of others, or as described earlier: the degree of enchantment is dependent on the 'degree of delight' it arouses in others. However, let's take the words of Brown and others who have made similar declarations at face value and examine the conditions under which passionate leadership can contribute to the cause of education and in the process arouse a 'degree of delight'.

Modelling enchanting leadership

Two models of relationships to be formed if passionate leadership is also to be enchanting leadership are proposed, illustrated in Figures 9.1 and 9.2. The model in Figure 9.1 refers to 'internal relationships' in that they are established in the immediate work environment of the leader. The model in Figure 9.2 refers to 'external relationships' because they require the leader to see 'a bigger picture' and make connections between education, economy and society.

Passion, trust and strategy

The 'internal relationships' modelled in Figure 9.1 indicate that passion by itself may amount to nothing more than a demonstration of self-indulgence, even if it is momentarily moving. For there to be enchanting leadership the leader must be trusted and there must be a credible strategy driven by a compelling vision that has high moral purpose.

Trust is a necessary element. Kotter (1990) considers leadership to be a four-part construct of establishing direction, aligning people, motivating and inspiring, and achieving change. Trust is important if alignment is to be achieved and people are to be motivated and inspired.

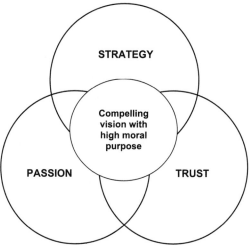

Figure 9.1: *The 'internal relationships' between passion, trust and strategy if leadership is to be enchanting*

Loss of trust has been a key theme in discourse on leadership in recent times, especially in respect to political leaders, although some writers contend that the loss is endemic. Fukuyama (1995) put this position in distinguishing between low-trust and high-trust societies, contending that 'Widespread distrust in a society ... imposes a kind of tax on all forms of economic activity; a tax that high-trust societies do not have to pay' (p. 28–9). Covey suggests that 'this low-trust tax is not only on economic activity, but on all activity – in every relationship, in every interaction, in every communication, in every decision, in every dimension of life' (Covey, 2006: 19).

Determining the extent to which there is a relationship between passion and trust is an interesting way to analyse the impact of policy and practice in education. In the United States, for example, the disparities in achievement between groups of students in different socio-economic or other demographic circumstances has aroused deep concern for several decades and various courses of action have been passionately proposed on both sides of politics. The *No Child Left Behind* legislation is a case in point. There is a high level of scepticism and suspicion in the profession on its efficacy and it is fair to say that levels of trust between policy makers and professionals are modest at best.

Credibility is an important aspect of trust when it comes to proposals for reform. Similar concerns to those underpinning *No Child Left Behind* have been raised in Australia. In 2000, a task force chaired by former minister for science, Barry Jones, and including current Prime Minister, Kevin Rudd, prepared a report that explained why and how Australia could become a 'Knowledge Nation'. Jones described it as 'a comprehensive policy framework linking those elements in Australia's society, economy and environment, especially human and physical resources, dependent on the generation, use and exchange of knowledge' (Jones, 2006: 455). The report was lampooned for its illustration in a 'mind map', an approach that is encouraged if not already commonplace in the nation's classrooms. It was given short shrift by Jones's leader Kim Beazley, who wanted to be remembered (if he won the election of 2001) as 'the education prime minister'. The strategies and networks proposed in Knowledge Nation amounted to an 'education revolution', which is the term now used by Kevin Rudd to describe what is needed in 2008 (Rudd eventually replaced Beazley as leader of the Labor Party). The lesson here is that there must be alignment of the emotions of passionate leaders and the symbols of trust if there is to be impact on policy and practice. As far as Figure 9.1 is concerned, there was passion and strategy but the level of trust (credibility) was not strong enough to sustain a Knowledge Nation.

No amount of passion or trust will suffice if well thought out strategies are not designed and delivered. Returning to the passion of Gordon Brown, his vision for education was replete with strategies for its realization, building on those of his predecessor Tony Blair, emphasizing parental engagement, 'real time' feedback on pupil progress, strengthening early childhood education, personalizing learning, expanding programmes for the gifted and talented, and raising the standards of teaching (Brown, 2007).

Figure 9.1 includes a 'compelling vision with high moral purpose'. The language has become clichéd in recent times but this should not distract from its substance. Brown's vision is that 'I want to see a Britain where every child can go to a world class school, supported by high aspirations, surrounded by excellent opportunities ... A Britain where effort is rewarded, ambition fulfilled, potential realised' (Brown, 2007). Elsewhere (Caldwell, 2006; Caldwell and Spinks, 2008) we propose a vision of change on the scale of transformation, defined as significant, systematic and sustained change that secures success for all students in all settings.

Figure 9.1 is presented as a Venn diagram to show the relationships among the three elements. Passionate leadership is ineffective if it does not engender trust. Those charged with implementation should be committed to the vision and the strategy. Passion, trust and strategy must be aligned with the vision. Alignment must be powerful if leadership is to be enchanting as well as passionate.

Education, economy and society

Figure 9.2 illustrates another set of relationships. They call for the leader to see a 'bigger picture' beyond the immediate work setting, connecting education, economy and society, hence their designation as 'external relationships'.

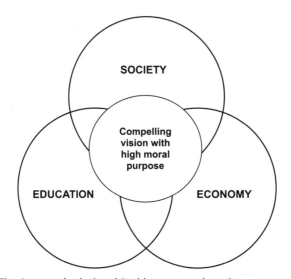

Figure 9.2: *The 'external relationships' between education, economy and society if leadership is to be enchanting*

Evidence of the need for these relationships may be seen in the lack of responsiveness in some quarters to legislation such as *No Child Left Behind* and the unrelenting regime of reform in some countries that focuses on literacy and numeracy and a requirement that schools deliver the skills base for an economy that must be sustained in an era of globalization. Gordon Brown illustrated the point in his vision for education: 'I make no apology for saying that education is the best economic policy. And I make no apology for wanting every child to be able to read, write and add up' (Brown, 2007). It seems that governments have never been more active in driving change and that claims of a passion for education on the part of ministers and prime ministers are often unrequited at the level of practice. This is not to say that there is no passion for leadership at the local level. It means that there is a disjunction of a kind that prevents passionate leadership being enchanting leadership.

The disjunction is illustrated in a statement that is often heard along the lines that 'I want to live in a society not an economy'. It may take some time for the disjunction to become a convergence of the kind illustrated in Figure 9.2 in which education is important for the well-being of society and the economy. A quality education and a strong economy help contribute to a vibrant society.

The convergence has been strong in the past. An example is the alignment of schools and society in an agricultural economy, a situation that continues to prevail in communities in many countries. A similar alignment was evident in industrial times to the point that the curriculum was determined to a large extent by the requirements of factories and management of education reflected a 'factory model'. Such an alignment is still important in many countries. New alignments are necessary for education in a knowledge economy in which the technologies of learning have been transformed.

Passionate leadership becomes enchanting leadership when two sets of relationships are established: those illustrated in Figure 9.2 that connect education, economy and society, and those illustrated in Figure 9.1, when a 'compelling vision with high moral purpose' is presented with passion, builds trust and is implemented in strategies that maintain the trust and realize the vision.

Are these two sets of relationships sufficient? The test is to return to the essence of enchantment. Have key stakeholders been roused to 'ecstatic admiration'? Has a 'degree of delight' been evoked? Culture is important and there is a role for education in creating and sustaining it. Gordon Brown addressed this to some extent in his vision which recognized that:

> ... *education has always been about more than exams, more than the basics, vital as they are. To educate is to form character, to shape values, and to liberate the imagination. It is to pass human wisdom, knowledge and ingenuity from one generation to the next. It is a duty and a calling. As Plutarch said, the mind is not a vessel to be filled but a fire to be kindled.* (Brown, 2007).

Enchanting leadership in action

Passionate leadership that is also enchanting leadership should ensure that these broader and richer features of education are addressed. It is inconceivable that such leadership can be exercised without these features being communicated in the words and actions of the leader. How this can be done may be illustrated by examining the ways particular leaders have gone about it, generally at the national level and specifically in the field of education. It should be noted that leadership in settings other than or broader than education require the adaptation of Figure 9.2 so that, for example, 'health' replaces 'education' for a leader in health.

Presidents and prime ministers

John F. Kennedy would be chosen by many to have illustrated 'enchanting leadership'. The legend of Camelot is invariably invoked to characterize his short presidency of the United States, being elected in the year of the first performance of the musical *Camelot* ('Don't let it be forgot, that once there was a spot, for one brief shining moment, that was known as Camelot'). The enchanting leadership of JFK lay more in the vision he offered and the symbol of hope he presented in the years of the Cold War. Some would say that the passion and pragmatics were more evident in another moment of enchanting leadership by Robert F. Kennedy, whose tilt at the presidency was cut short by assassination. Martin Luther King provided enchanting leadership to the extent that each element in Figures 9.1 and 9.2 was evident in the civil rights movement that was inspired by his words and actions.

Shortly after these examples of enchanting leadership in the United States was that in Canada by Pierre Elliott Trudeau, especially in the early years of his prime ministership in the late 1960s and early 1970s. It was observed at first hand by the author when resident in Canada between 1968 and 1981. Trudeau was a French-Canadian intellectual who captured the hearts and minds of the people with his vision of a 'just society', a united Canada and a style that suited the informality of the times, often seen to be poking fun at the trappings of power and privilege. He proved resolute in the face of the Quebec separatist movement, notably during the kidnapping and murder of a cabinet minister. More moments of 'ecstatic admiration' occurred when he married an attractive young woman about 30 years his junior. The relationships illustrated in Figures 9.1 and 9.2 were evident for a time, including strategies to support the roll-out of bilingual education across the country. The enchanting times came to an end and he suffered electoral defeat. A political resurrection and a second stint as prime minister made little difference, even though his leadership continued to be important in efforts to maintain national unity. Trudeau failed to adopt strategies to sustain the economy and there was a shift in societal expectations of leadership style.

From the early 1960s and continuing to the present has been the enchanting leadership of Nelson Mandela. 'Compelling vision with high moral purpose' was evident from the outset, sustained through decades of imprisonment, moving to an even higher plane in an astonishing strategy for reconciliation and harmony when he gained his freedom and won the presidency. Passion, trust and strategy were aligned, as illustrated in Figure 9.1. Education, as well as other fields of public endeavour, economy and society was aligned, as illustrated in Figure 9.2, including strategies for schools to promote reconciliation and harmony as well as to develop the skills for an economy that would support a society that honoured these values.

How do these reflections help us understand leadership that is enchanting as well in passionate? Accepting that the leadership in each instance was (is) enchanting; we learn that passion by itself is not enough. It must be channelled to a cause that the leader is able to articulate through words and actions, communicating what was described earlier as 'compelling vision with high moral purpose'. These were leaders at the national level and it was a wide constituency whose trust had to be won. Credible strategies were a source of this trust as well as necessary for the vision to be realized. Winning 'ecstatic admiration' or engendering a 'degree of delight' among others (constituents) is the essence of enchantment. Words and actions were important, but these were idiosyncratic. Each was (is) a charismatic leader but, as noted by Collins (2001) in *Good to Great*, charisma is not essential. Each leader could see a 'bigger picture', achieving the connections between education, economy and society (or similar synergy) in different ways in different settings. Context is important. Enchantment may not last if the 'bigger picture' changes and the leader does not or cannot adapt (this was the case with Trudeau).

Leaders in education

These understandings apply also to leadership in education. Winning 'ecstatic admiration' or engendering a 'degree of delight' call for different kinds of words and actions on the part of the leader. In that respect the task is a little easier for the leader in education is seen by or works with others on almost a daily basis, whereas leaders at the national level who must work across many fields must use a variety of media to communicate vision and win trust. There is no one best way to go about the task so the particular words and actions will be idiosyncratic. Charisma is important but it is not necessary, as noted by Collins in describing the Level 5 'executive leader' who acts 'with quiet, calm determination; relies principally on inspired standards, not inspiring charisma to motivate' (Collins, 2001: 36).

Collins's conclusion about charisma is affirmed by Brighouse. Writing about passionate leadership for the National College for School Leadership, he observed that:

> *Leadership style is very frequently misunderstood, especially when it comes to passionate leadership. It is wrongly assumed that such leadership – indeed sometimes all leadership – has to be 'charismatic'. Nothing could be further from the truth ... Many deeds are quiet, cumulative and private rather than grand and public ... Wherever leaders are on the spectrum from quiet and understated to flamboyant, they will be good with language and, especially, with imagery which captures the imagination of the community they serve.* (Brighouse, 2001)

Tim Brighouse has served in a range of leadership positions in education, perhaps most notably as the Chief Education Officer in Birmingham (1993–2002). There would likely be universal agreement that his leadership was (and continues to be) enchanting. Indeed, this was part of the headline over a newspaper account of his work (Wilby, 2007). Brighouse, it proclaimed, 'has made a career out of enchanting teachers and bamboozling critics'. Wilby cited advice by Brighouse to 'spend two hours a week doing "acts of unexpected kindness", remembering birthdays and writing appreciative notes'. 'Ecstatic admiration' is an accurate way to describe the response to such actions. Brighouse's leadership models the passion–trust–strategy relationship illustrated in Figure 9.1. An illustration cited by Wilby was Brighouse's decision not to publish league tables of school results in Birmingham (although schools were told how their results compared to schools in similar settings). Wilby reported that the schools 'agreed to set their own targets, possibly because, as Woodhead [former Chief Inspector of Schools] argued, they could then legitimize mediocrity, but more probably because it was Brighouse asking them to do it'. Headteachers and teachers trusted his passion and trusted his strategies. The outcome was an improvement in student achievement across the system.

Enchanting leadership and the transformation of schools

The final issue to be addressed is whether the view of enchanting leadership presented in this chapter can be accommodated in a broader view of change in education. The framework in *Raising the Stakes: From Improvement to Transformation in the Reform of Schools* (Caldwell and Spinks, 2008), as illustrated in Figure 9.3, is offered as a guide. An explanation of the key concepts and short account of how the framework was developed is followed by a description of the role of the leader and, for our current purposes, how passionate leadership that is also enchanting strengthens the framework.

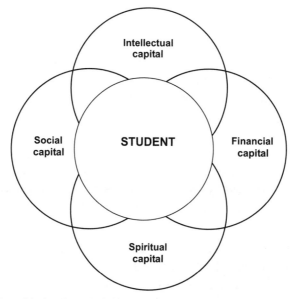

Figure 9.3: *Four kinds of capital that contribute to the transformation of schools* (adapted from Caldwell and Spinks, 2008: 33)

Key concepts

The framework identifies four sets of resources, described as capital, which must be strong and aligned if transformation is to be achieved. Transformation is considered to be significant, systematic and sustained change that secures success for all students in all settings. The focus in Figure 9.3 is therefore the student. The four forms of capital are defined as follows:

- *Intellectual capital* refers to the level of knowledge and skill of those who work in or for the school.
- *Social capital* refers to the strength of formal and informal partnerships and networks involving the school, parents, community, business and industry, indeed all individuals, agencies, organizations and institutions that have the potential to support and be supported by the school.
- *Spiritual capital* refers to the strength of moral purpose and the degree of coherence among values, beliefs and attitudes about life and learning. For some schools, spiritual capital has a foundation in religion. In other schools, spiritual capital may refer to ethics and values shared by members of the school and its community.
- *Financial capital* refers to the monetary resources available to support the school.

The four kinds of capital are shown as intersecting rather than discrete sets because each contributes to the others. For example, the knowledge and skill of members of the community including parents (social capital) may contribute to the knowledge and skill available to the school (intellectual capital). Values and beliefs about life and learning (spiritual capital) are factors that help determine the social capital of the school. Money (financial capital) is necessary but much depends on how funds are deployed, including the extent to which they help build the knowledge and skill of teachers (intellectual capital).

The importance of intellectual capital was given worldwide prominence in a report by McKinsey and Company (Barber and Mourshed, 2007) that examined 'how the world's best-performing school systems come out on top'. Particular attention was given to Canada, Finland, Singapore, South Korea and some districts in the

United States (notably Boston and Chicago). It found that:

The experience of these top school systems suggests that three things matter most: (1) getting the right people to become teachers, (2) developing them into effective instructors and, (3) ensuring that the system is able to deliver the best instruction for every child. (Barber and Mourshed, 2007: Executive summary)

Creating the framework

The framework in Figure 9.3 was developed and tested over three years from 2005 to 2007. An innovative approach utilized case studies (49), master classes (4) and workshops (60) involving school and school system leaders in 11 countries where there was an agenda for or interest in transformation and where school self-management was well-established or in the early stages of implementation. Forty of the 49 case studies were contributed by school leaders in 13 of the 60 workshops. Several workshops were incorporated in conferences and postgraduate programmes in leadership and management.

A feature of most of the workshops was the invitation to school and school system leaders to respond to key questions on design, implementation, issues and outcomes of efforts to achieve the transformation of schools. An interactive computer-based technology enabled large numbers of individual and group responses to be gathered for subsequent analysis. The interactive technology was utilized in 50 out of a total of 60 workshops, with approximately 2,500 participants generating more than 10,000 responses for subsequent analysis. Five of the 60 workshops considered the concept of 'exhilarating leadership' and the findings, including an analysis of responses generated with the interactive technology, were reported in the first section of the chapter.

More detailed accounts of the three-year research and development project are contained in *Re-imagining Educational Leadership* (Caldwell, 2006) and *Raising the Stakes: From Improvement to Transformation in the Reform of Schools* (Caldwell and Spinks, 2008). Further work was underway at the time of writing, with the framework in Figure 9.3 the starting point for case studies of capital formation in high-performing secondary schools in six countries (Australia, China, England, Finland, United States and Wales).

Enchanting leadership as capital in the transformation of schools

It is not by random effort that the four kinds of capital become strong and aligned. Outstanding governance is required. Discussions about governance are often limited to the importance of clear specification of the roles and responsibilities of different stakeholders. This is necessary but the overall purpose of governance should not be overlooked. Consistent with the model in Figure 9.3, governance is defined as the process through which the school builds its intellectual, social, financial and spiritual capital and aligns them to achieve its goals.

Leadership and management are important considerations and it is in this context that passionate leadership that is also enchanting leadership may be viewed as capital in its own right, contributing to and often energizing the four kinds of capital in Figure 9.3. Brighouse (2001) believes that at 'the heart of successful leadership must be a passion for learning' and he included professional learning on the part of teachers and their leaders as well as learning for students 'as all take part in a shared and never-ending journey of learning'.

A striking example of how passion in leadership contributes to the formation of capital is presented in the Australian setting in the experience of the leadership of John Fleming, first as headteacher (principal) of Bellfield Primary School and then as Head of the Edrington campus of Haileybury College (both schools are in Melbourne). Bellfield is a state school located in a low socio-economic community where there are high levels of unemployment, single-parent families and drug and alcohol abuse. Under Fleming's leadership the percentage of students in Grade 1 reading with 100 per cent accuracy at the target level rose from 34.6 per cent in 1998 to 100 per cent in 2004. The key to success was building the capacity of staff to deliver the kind of instruction that was needed (intellectual capital) which involved changing the beliefs of staff about the capacity of all students to succeed (spiritual capital) and strengthening the engagement of parents in supporting the work of the school (social capital). The school was funded on the same basis as schools in similar socio-economic circumstances (financial capital) but only 26.3 per cent of students in the latter could read with 100 per cent accuracy in 2004. Along with several of his leadership team Fleming moved to Haileybury, a government-subsidised private school, in 2006 and led a similar transformation in reading instruction to the extent that students at the Edrington campus were significantly outperforming their counterparts on the other two campuses of the school within two years.

Fleming has written an account of what occurred at Bellfield and of progress at Haileybury (Fleming and Kleinhenz, 2007) which includes a description of his approach to leadership. He believes there are three important attributes – passion, determination and vision: 'The entire staff needs to witness your passion for education and your desire for school improvement' and 'your determination that the processes implemented will make a difference and that you can achieve your goals as a school' (Fleming and Kleinhenz, 2007: 85).

Teachers at both schools were challenged to make the changes described above. However, consistent with Figure 9.1, passion alone was not sufficient; trust and strategy were critical to success. As Fleming acknowledges: 'Staff found the process daunting until they experienced it. Once credibility and trust had been established, the teachers found the process affirming' (Fleming and Kleinhenz, 2007: 76). Fleming would disavow any suggestion that his leadership was enchanting to the point that his colleagues were moved to 'ecstatic admiration'. He goes out of his way to pay tribute to his leadership team and staff at the school (see also the account of his leadership in Caldwell, 2006). However, it is apparent that staff morale was high even though the experience was daunting. Between 1996 and 2005 no full-time member of staff sought to leave Bellfield for reasons other than promotion (Fleming and Kleinhenz, 2007: 63).

Summary

There would be few who disagree with the proposition that leaders in education should find the experience to be enchanting: better to be enchanted than disenchanted. There are too many accounts of disenchanted leaders. The limited research on the theme is consistent in finding that enchantment is an emotional response to working well with others and achieving great outcomes. It depends on the response of others as well as the response of self. While we would wish for more leaders to find the experience enchanting, it would be even better if those with whom they work were also enchanted. The line of argument in this chapter acknowledged the nuanced distinction between 'enchanted leadership' and 'enchanting leadership'. In its strongest form, enchanting leadership engenders 'ecstatic admiration' and a 'degree of delight' in those with whom the leader works.

Passion by itself may not lead to these outcomes. Passion by itself may be no more than an exercise in self-indulgence. Seeking the 'ecstatic admiration' by others for its own sake is a vanity as well as self-indulgence. If the intention is to realize a 'compelling vision with high moral purpose' such as securing success for all students in all settings, then passion must engender trust in others and be accompanied by credible strategies, as modelled in Figure 9.1. If a big-picture perspective is adopted and a broader, long-term, sustainable vision is to be realized, then enchanting leadership reflects a well-understood synergy of education, economy and society, as modelled in Figure 9.2. These relationships were illustrated in accounts of enchanting leadership in different settings.

There is compelling evidence that the transformation of schools calls for strength in and alignment of four kinds of resources: intellectual capital, social capital, spiritual capital and financial capital. Enchanting leadership is a particular resource that can contribute to if not energize each of these.

The integrating force in all of these matters is trust. The impact of passion in leadership can be strengthened or weakened to the extent that there is trust. This is an underlying theme of Stephen Covey writing in *The Speed of Trust* (Covey, 2006).

There is one thing that is common to every individual, relationship, team, family, organisation, nation, economy, and civilisation throughout the world – one thing which, if removed, will destroy the most powerful government, the most successful business, the most thriving economy, the most influential leadership, the greatest friend-

ship, the strongest character, the deepest love.

On the other hand, if developed and leveraged, that one thing has the potential to create unparalleled success and prosperity in every dimension of life. Yet it is the least understood, most neglected, and most underestimated possibility of our time.

That one thing is trust. (Covey, 2006: 1)

We should add the school or the system of education to Covey's list. Trust is the key to enchanted leadership.

References

Barber, M. and Mourshed, M. (2007) *How the World's Best-Performing School Systems Come Out on Top*. London: McKinsey & Company.

Brighouse, T. (2001). *Passionate Leadership*, invited paper in a series providing an evidence base for leadership. Nottingham: National College for School Leadership (www.ncsl.org.uk/media/889/36/passionate-leadership.pdf: accessed 7 November 2007).

Brown, G. (2007). 'Vision for Education', speech at the University of Greenwich, 31 October (www.labour.org.uk/gordon_brown_sets_out_his_vision_for_education accessed 7 November 2007).

Caldwell, B. J. (2006) *Re-imagining Educational Leadership*. Camberwell: ACER Press, and London: Sage.

Caldwell, B. J. and Spinks, J. M. (2008) *Raising the Stakes: From Improvement to Transformation in the Reform of Schools*. London: Routledge.

Collins, J. (2001) *Good to Great*. London: Random House.

Covey, S. (2006) *The Speed of Trust*,.New York: Simon & Schuster.

Day, C. and Bakioglu, A. (1996) 'Development and disenchantment in the professional lives of headteachers', in Goodson, I. and Hargreaves, A. (eds) *Teachers' Professional Lives*. London: Falmer.

Fleming, J. and Kleinhenz, E. (2007) *Towards a* Moving *School: Developing a Professional Learning and Performance Culture*, Camberwell: ACER Press.

Fukuyama, F. (1995) *Trust: The Social Virtues and the Creation of Prosperity*. New York: The Free Press.

Jones, B. (2006) *A Thinking Reed*. Crows Nest, NSW: Allen & Unwin.

Kotter, J. P. (1990) *A Force for Change: How Leadership Differs from Management*. New York: The Free Press.

Wilby, P. (2007) 'The secrets of Saint Tim', *Education Guardian*, 24 April.
Woods, R. (2002) *Enchanted Headteachers: Sustainability in Primary School Headship*, a Practitioner Enquiry Report of the National College for School Leadership, Nottingham: NCSL (www.ncsl.org.uk/media/DCB/18/enchanting-headteachers.pdf: accessed 23 December 2007).

Conclusion

Brent Davies

This book has been structured in five major sections.

- The first section is concerned with defining the passionate teacher, the passionate leader and the passionate school, with the core chapter by Tim Brighouse.
- The second section centres on passion and educational leadership, with chapters from John Novak and Alan Flintham.
- The third section looks at research on passionate leadership, with chapters from Chris Day and Brent Davies.
- The fourth section considers passionate leadership for schools and teachers, with chapters from John MacBeath and Andy Hargreaves.
- The fifth section centres on defining the work of passionate leaders and building a model for passionate leadership, with chapters from Geoff Southworth and Brian Caldwell.

What are the insights that can be drawn from this collective set of work and ideas? Certainly this is not a blueprint for educational leadership or some easily applied set of formulae for improving leadership and schools. What it is is an opportunity to stand back from the managerialist obsession with leadership being concerned with outcomes of test results and easily produced data. This book provides an opportunity to reflect on the core moral purpose of education to engage the human expression of hope and the chance to make a difference to children's lives through developing a passion for learning and a passion for social justice. Lee Bolman and Terry Deal's book *Leading with Soul* (1995) talks about those leadership characteristics and virtues that go beyond competence and skills to those that involve the human heart and try to improve and give something of oneself to the world. We often ignore this dimension in the technical approach of breaking down the elements of leadership and forgetting the intangibles and non-quantifiable assets and contributions that individuals can make. Indeed, Terry Deal and Ken Peterson in *Shaping School Culture* (1999) see school leaders taking on eight symbolic roles:

1. Historian – understanding where the school has come from and why it behaves currently as it does.
2. Anthropological sleuth – seeks to understand the current set of norms, values and beliefs that define the current culture.
3. Visionary – works with others to define a deeply value-focused picture of the future for the school.
4. Symbolic – affirms values through dress, behaviour, attention and routines.
5. Potter – shapes and is shaped by the school's heroes, rituals, traditions, ceremonies, symbols; brings in staff who share core values.
6. Poet – uses language to reinforce values and sustains the school's best image of itself.
7. Actor – improvises in the school's inevitable dramas, comedies and tragedies.
8. Healer – oversees transitions and changes in the life of the school; heals wounds of conflict and loss.

This categorization demonstrates how leaders move beyond the technical part of the role to the people and emotional part of the leadership mystique. I believe it is the passion of leaders for their role and the courage to meet challenges that enables them to achieve both their functional and managerial tasks as well as undertaking these symbolic roles. What have the five sections of the book been able to do to provide insights into this passionate leadership?

In section one, Tim Brighouse provides a powerful articulation that passion is linked to educational beliefs. In Figure 1.1, (page 18) his 'beliefs of passionate and outstanding teachers' together with 'habits and behaviours of passionate and outstanding teachers' is a remarkable agenda for transformation of learning and schools by passionate and committed individuals. This should form the professional development agenda of schools as it clearly articulates what it means to be 'outstanding'. These two items in Figure 1.1 represent both high-level skills and beliefs that can only be ignited by the passion for learning and teaching. They highlight the difference that values and beliefs can make to children. These items provide a template for teacher development. Tim's mantras for passionate headteachers:

- providing a credible example as learner and teacher;
- being an effective and inspiring storyteller and expert enthusiastic questioner;
- mastering the advanced skills of delegation and encouraging 'risk takers';
- creating capacity and energy among staff;
- seeking and charting improvement and constantly extending the vision;
- meeting and minimizing crisis and securing the environment;

similarly provides a template for leadership development that builds great leadership. The final point he makes in his chapter regarding passionate schools is that they are 'striving for success for all pupils and staff rather than acting on the assumption that the reverse side of the success coin has to involve failure for some, and believing that talent/intelligence is multi-faceted and powerfully affected by the environment' is an excellent frame of reference for passionate leadership.

In section two, we have two views on leadership. John Novak builds a case for passionate invitational leadership and Alan Flintham considers how that leadership can be sustained and, where necessary, restored. Both look at the challenge of sustaining leadership and the passion that drives it. This is a much neglected area. While leaders support and nurture others, who supports and nurture the leaders themselves? Alan looks at belief networks, support networks and external networks as means of re-igniting the passion and sustaining headteachers. John uses the concept of inviting oneself and others personally and professionally as a means of constant regeneration and renewal. What these two powerful chapters do is highlight the absolute necessity of both actively sustaining and renewing the passion in leadership. The lesson for leaders is that they have to look after themselves so as to look after others. Passion for education, for learning and for children brings individuals into teaching and when they move on to leadership roles those initial passions have to be sustained, and the corrosive effect of the organization 'wear and tear' needs to be confronted and resolved if we are to have leaders who are to inspire the next generation of learners.

In section three, Chris Day and Brent Davies report on outstanding leaders who by their passion for learning and their wish to transform the lives of children in their care have made remarkable efforts to create successful schools. The lesson from these two chapters is the ability of leaders to shape and change organizations by their values and the passion. For this change to occur, it is necessary to turn those values into processes and actions. Notably they both see passion in itself of little value unless it is about seeking transformation and achievement for children so that the school 'can make a difference'. This passion is strongly linked to a values-driven agenda and the moral purpose of schooling. It is important to recognize that caring, collaborating and being committed, while good in themselves, are for the purpose of achievement and success in its various forms. Refocusing and revisiting values and purpose should be part of the personal and professional review process of leaders.

In section four, the chapters by John MacBeath and Andy Hargreaves consider how passionate leadership impacts on schools and teachers. Both chapters argue that passionate leadership is about deep learning that affects children's understanding and lives. John argues that the managerial frameworks of targets, planning, evaluation and inspection need to be construed by passionate leaders for what they believe in and that passionate leadership is courageous leadership to construe these things in a sometimes subversive way to establish sustainable educational development. Andy at times takes an anti-leadership stance and looks at passionate leadership from a teacher perspective. Both these chapters argue that passionate leaders put learning and children at the centre of school improvement and reform.

In the final section, Geoff Southworth and Brian Caldwell looked at the emerging nature of passionate leadership. Geoff builds an account of the work of leaders and moves on to argue that a leader's values and passions are what drives and sustains them. To him, values provide meaning to actions, and the passion to contribute to a larger purpose makes sense of daily experience. Brian took on this theme by using the concept of 'enchanted leadership' as a means of exploring passionate leadership. He puts forward the case that for the transformation of schools, four types of capital are required: intellectual capital, social capital, spiritual capital and financial capital. He argues that enchanting leadership can contribute to energizing each of these for effective transformation. The elements of enchanting leadership which readers might reflect on are those of strategy, passion and trust coming together with a compelling vision based on high moral purpose.

What do passionate leaders do? The book has provided a number of perspectives and insights and I would like draw some of these ideas together.

First, passionate leaders articulate the vision. Passionate leadership is about a deep-rooted belief in better opportunities and alternative outcomes. The ability to conceptualize those new futures and communicate them in a clear and concise way is vital. A vision should connect to the reality of the individuals in the organization's current experience as well as the hope and aspirations for the future. In essence, it has to connect to the heart as well as the head. The ability also to convey both the sense of importance and urgency of the journey to new and better futures is critical. It will only happen of course if others have faith and trust that the leader can achieve the change and that all those in the organization are involved in the process and outcomes so that they can commit to the vision.

Second, passionate leaders share the values. They move beyond the vision and mission statements and not only articulate values in written statements and programmes, but also in their everyday speech and interactions. Invitational leadership highlights how each and every person is valuable and important. In the education publishing world I am immensely saddened by the series of books entitled 'Getting the Buggers to: ... "learn" ... "do their home work" ... "read"' – is that how we think of children? Are they not unique creations with individual capabilities? How passionate leaders talk about children, colleagues and the school demonstrates their deep-seated values. How values are expressed and lived in day-to-day speech is vital if passionate leaders are to create a shared sense of moral purpose.

Third, passionate leaders set examples and standards that are possible. They convince people, by their personal standards, of what can be achieved and they behave ethically. They set clear goals that are achievable and encourage students and staff to meet them. They move beyond glib sayings such as 'raising the bar' and 'narrowing the gap'. This year, standing outside the Olympic Museum in Lausanne, I walked under the men's high jump bar (set at the record height). I certainly could not jump it and raising it would not be an incentive to try! So what are achievable and meaningful success criteria? Setting targets that 85 per cent of our children can be above average shows little understanding of the mathematical concept of average! Better that 100 per cent of our children can achieve their individual learning targets.

Fourth, passionate leaders are committed for the long term. They build in sustainable approaches to learning and organizational development. They have a belief system that all children can achieve and that all children will achieve. Data is a key factor here. I would prefer the expression 'data informed' to 'data driven'. Data driven suggests that we react to short-term numerical results and bend all our efforts in that direction. Data informed means we use quantitative data as indicative information but also balance it with qualitative insights about a child's many talents. Information and judgement are necessary to build an holistic picture of a child's progress in order to develop strategies and approaches to enhance deep learning.

Fifth, passionate leaders care. They care in a positive way, 'care to make a difference' and 'care to challenge'. They care for the person and support pupils, teachers and parents in their roles as individuals and in their educational roles. Care can be considered as 'soft' and 'easy going' but real care both looks after the person as an individual and challenges their performance, attitude and commitment. Moving from a comfortable and adequate environment to one of high achievement and challenge often involves personal and professional challenge. That takes courage not to accept the status quo. Moving from a 'cruising' or 'strolling' school to a high achieving school can be as difficult a journey as moving from failure to satisfactory. Thus passionate leaders are courageous leaders, because they have the courage to challenge. This is a major factor in turning passion into action.

Six, passionate leaders celebrate. They celebrate achievements and success in the broadest sense. How individuals learn, socialize, contribute to society and make moral judgements are all areas for celebration and recognition. Believing that learning and education is hard work as well as enjoyable and fun is part of the positive outlook they develop. The culture of the school should be bringing out the best in everyone and celebrating when we do so. Passionate leaders create ceremonies and traditions as formal means of celebration. Most significantly, in their daily acts of recognition and kindness, they celebrate their colleagues' and students' achievements. How we engage in the learning journey as a process of commitment and passion should be a major reason for celebration and success.

Finally, passionate leaders are driven because it matters; it matters to them that they make a difference!

In conclusion, bringing together such a distinguished set of contributors has helped re-ignite my passion for my leadership work by drawing on wonderful insights and perspectives from the leaders who have written so eloquently in this book.

References

Bolman, L. and Deal, T.E. (1995) *Leading with Soul*. San Francisco, CA: Jossey-Bass.

Deal, T.E. and Petersen, K.D. (1999) *Shaping School Culture*. San Francisco, CA: Jossey-Bass.

Index